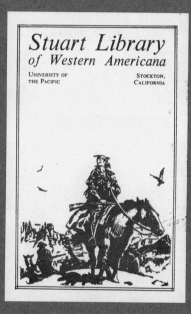

The Early Temples of the Mormons

The Early Temples of the Mormons

The Architecture of the Millennial Kingdom in the American West

Laurel B. Andrew

State University of New York Press Albany 1978

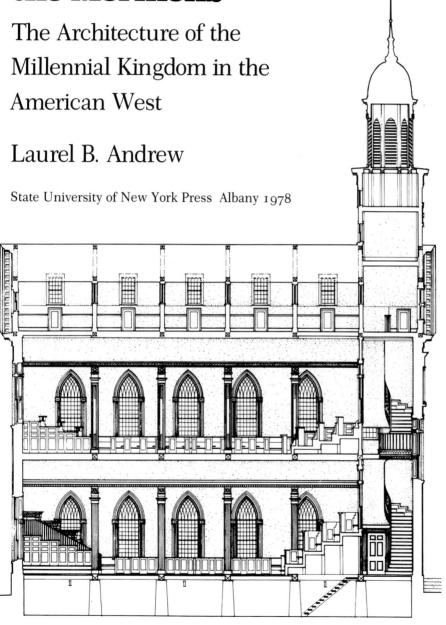

First published in 1978 by
State University of New York Press
Albany, New York 12246

Printed and made in the United States of America

Library of Congress Cataloging in Publication Data

Andrew, Laurel B
  The early temples of the Mormons.

  Includes bibliographical references.
  1. Temples, Mormon.   I. Title.
NA4829.M67A53   726'.58'9373   77-23971
ISBN 0-87395-358-4

Contents

Illustrations

Acknowledgments

Among the many who have assisted me, I should like to give special thanks to the staff of the Historical Department of The Church of Jesus Christ of Latter-day Saints for providing me with a wealth of primary source material upon which to draw and for permission to photograph many drawings. The members of my doctoral committee at the University of Michigan, T. Edgar Lyon of Nauvoo Restoration, Inc., and James Mac Crea of The Church of Jesus Christ of Latter-day Saints Architectural Department gave me valuable suggestions and encouragement.

Without the constant support, critical advice, and photographic expertise of my husband, David S. Andrew, the preparation of this manuscript would not have been nearly as interesting and personally rewarding as it has been.

Figure 2 drawn by L. J. List

Figures 3, 4, 5, 6, 81, 82 courtesy of The Church of Jesus Christ of Latter-day Saints

Figures 7, 8, 10, 25, 26, 27, 34, 40, 42, 43, 45, 49, 50, 51, 52, 53, 54, 55, 56, 63, 64, 65, 73, 75, 76, 77, 78, 79, 82, 83, 84, 85, 86, 87, 88, 89, 90 photographed by David S. Andrew

Figures 9, 13, 20, 22, 70, 76, 80 courtesy of the Utah State Historical Society

Figures 11, 12, 19, 21, 23, 36, 37, 38, 39, 41, 44, 46, 47, 48, 50, 58, 59, 60, 67, 71, 72, 84 reproduced with the permission of the Historical Department, The Church of Jesus Christ of Latter-day Saints

Figures 14, 17, 18 produced by Audio-Visual Services, Reorganized Church of Jesus Christ of Latter Day Saints

Figure 15 courtesy of the Library of Congress, Historic American Buildings Survey

Figures 24 and 32 courtesy of the Missouri Historical Society

Figure 33 reproduced with the permission of The George N. Meissner Memorial Rare Book Department, Washington University Libraries, St. Louis, Missouri

Chapter 1

The Origins of Mormonism in Nineteenth-Century America

The Latter-day Saints, or Mormons, are known to non-Mormons primarily for their earnest young missionaries, the Tabernacle Choir with its performances of the old favorites of religious and patriotic music, and their strict abjuration of tobacco, alcoholic beverages, and stimulants like coffee and tea. On a cross-country drive, some may recall having seen the temple in Salt Lake City, a battlemented granite edifice whose imposing presence attests to the continuing vitality of Mormonism in Utah. Politically conservative, feeling no need to embrace ecumenism, and espousing, as it does, traditional American values, the Mormon Church impresses one as a zealous fundamentalist Protestant sect, whose attitudes are well expressed by this solid, austere temple.

Theologically, however, Mormonism is something of an anomaly among established American religions. Though it officially abandoned its most notorious practice, polygamy, in the late nineteenth century, its dogma is distinctive enough to make it a religion unto itself rather than a mere denomination. With its belief in the plurality of gods (and man's potential for becoming a god himself), continuous revelation, celestial marriage, elaborate vicarious work for the dead, and its denial of the concept of original sin, Mormonism is decidedly not an orthodox form of Protestantism. In fact, its relationship to traditional Christianity is uncertain, for Latter-day Saints also reject the idea of a triune, spiritual deity, believing that God the Father, Christ, and the Holy Spirit are three separate, physical beings, and hold that man has a premortal existence as a spirit as well as a resurrected soul and body. The formulation of these and other unconventional doctrines within the period of a few decades in mid-nineteenth-century America was accompanied by the creation of a thriving, aggressively independent, utopian society with its own values and cultural mores. The Latter-day Saints have now been assimilated into American life, becoming in the process something rather different from what they were in the past, but their singular beliefs remain to set them apart and suggest the origins of their religious heritage.

Although unique today, Mormonism in its infancy was only one of a

1. Whitney Cross, *The Burned-Over District: The Social and Intellectual History of Enthusiastic Religion in Western New York* (Ithaca, 1950), p. 199.
2. *Ibid.*, p. 3.

variety of eccentric revivalist sects which sprang up along the westward migration route in upper New York state. A broad belt of territory following the Erie Canal, the "Burned-over District" was so termed in the decades between 1820 and 1850 because of the succession of emotional religious revivals, usually short-lived, which swept through the area, leaving the participants exhausted until the onslaught of the next wave. These were the more extreme manifestations of a general revival of religion in the young republic known as the Second Great Awakening, so extreme that circuit-riding preachers of established denominations complained that the susceptibility of this particular region to fervent and unorthodox religion left it unreceptive to their own ministrations. Palmyra, the home of Mormonism's founder, Joseph Smith, was in the center of the Burned-over District.

Western New York was populous, but also unstable, as emigrants from New England who had settled there moved on into the cheaper lands of the Western Reserve. On the edge of the frontier, though too civilized to be really a part of it, this territory experienced a burst of prosperity with the completion of the Erie Canal in 1825. The new wealth and rapid rise in land value which the Canal produced inspired unbounded faith in the future of the region, and encouraged intense patriotic feelings associated with the belief that America was the greatest and most perfect of nations. "The dogma of American democracy, vigorously rising in Jacksonian days, contained a supreme optimism, a belief in the ultimate perfection of society through progressive improvement in humankind."[1] Religious revivals provided not only a focal point for social intercourse and community entertainment, but were also an expression of this democratic bias and prevailing faith in the future, for religious enthusiasm was channelled into "crusades aimed at the perfection of mankind and the attainment of millennial happiness" for all men.[2]

Almost all of the peripheral sects of western New York professed some sort of expectation of an early millennium, the thousand-year earthly reign of Christ which would culminate in the Last Judgment, the end of the world, and the final triumph of good over evil. Most were not as specific as William Miller, who in 1830 proclaimed that the Second Coming and the inauguration of the millennium would take place in March 1843, but the conviction of its imminence permeated all levels of society. The more extreme expected a literal reign of Christ and the transformation of the earth by supernatural occurrences. Millenarian sects like the Shakers and Millerites withdrew from the secular world to prepare for the cataclysmic events of the Apocalypse, and even those who regarded the millennium allegorically felt that the world was in the last stage of historic time and that a utopian age was about to begin which would see great advances in political and social progress. A belief in the inevitable triumph of Christian principles and the consequent emergence of a religious utopia was a basic tenet of many Protestant churches. Nonreligious movements were also affected by such hopes, according to some scholars. Temperance crusades, abolitionism and others thrived on millennial expectations.

Related to the millennial sects and to the constellation of ideas generated by them were the Perfectionists. Reverberations of John Humphrey Noyes's Perfectionist movement were felt in the Burned-over District for some time before their major community was set up in 1847 at Oneida, New York. A scattering of Perfectionist groups was present throughout central New York during this era of revivals and reached a height of popularity about 1834. Noyes held that the Second Coming had already occurred in 70 A.D. and that the benefits it made possible had now to be implemented by the establishment of egalitarian, communistic societies. Believing that they were without sin, the Perfectionists avoided conventional social practices like monogamy in favor of "complex marriage," in which all were considered married to one another, and a particular marriage to one person lasted only a few weeks or months before another partner was taken. Perfectionists attempted to live in absolute harmony while expediting the arrival of the perfect society through the creation of a biologically and morally superior man via eugenic experimentation.

The Yankee independence and individualism characteristic of these settlers from rural New England had a religious analogue in their belief that one need only "know" the will of God to found new sects or to radically alter traditional Christian concepts. Thus, when Joseph Smith asserted in 1830 that he possessed a new scripture commensurate in authority with the Old and New Testaments, he took his place among several popular leaders professing divine revelation, if not divinity itself. The Shakers' late-eighteenth-century prophetess, Mother Ann Lee, had claimed to embody in the flesh the feminine aspect of a bisexual God and as such represented the Second Coming. The Shakers, one colony of whom resided in Sodus Bay, New York, only thirty miles from Palmyra, expressed their personal experiencing of God in hypnotic dancing and "speaking in tongues." Mother Ann reinterpreted original sin as having been sexual intercourse and insisted upon strict celibacy in the Shaker communities. Jemima Wilkinson, believing that she was Christ, presided over the celibate, communistic Community of the Publick Universal Friend, only twenty-five miles from Palmyra, at Jerusalem, New York.

Even traditional denominations were subject to upheavals in the Burned-over District. Renegade factions split the Baptists into Reformed Baptists, Hard-Shell Baptists, Free-Will Baptists, Footwashers, etc., all rejecting the authority of the eastern congregations. The religious revivalism of the early nineteenth century has been interpreted as a "rebellion of western democracy against an aristocratic theology that seemed to imply the existence of a small elite of chosen men, a proclamation of pioneer self-help and effort against the notion of elec-

3. Thomas F. O'Dea, *The Mormons* (Chicago, 1957), p. 18.

tion. . . ."[3] Most preachers were unschooled evangelists and itinerant faith-healers, whose open-air camp meetings were undisciplined affairs, involving shouting, singing, conversion, and sometimes mass hysteria. It was from this tolerant, open, and experimental society that Mormonism emerged.

The basis of the Church of Christ, renamed Church of Jesus Christ of Latter-day Saints in 1838, was the Book of Mormon. In 1827 twenty-two-year-old Joseph Smith was led by Moroni, an angel of the Lord, to a hill a short distance from the Smith farm, located between Palmyra and Manchester. There he unearthed a box containing golden plates with writing of an unknown language upon them. These he "translated" between 1827 and 1830 with the aid of some magic seer stones provided by the Lord for this purpose and found that the plates contained the record of an ancient American civilization. When the translation was completed the angel returned and took the plates up into heaven. In essence the Book of Mormon, as Smith called his translation, was a New World scripture which indicated an American religious and historical tradition independent of the European and Near Eastern past. The golden plates recorded the history of the New World Indians and explained their origin, a subject of much interest and speculation in the early nineteenth century. Theories concerning their origin were rampant and focussed in particular on the strange burial mounds which dotted the landscape of the eastern United States. Numerous writers hypothetically reconstructed a lost race of "mound builders" and suggested that the founders of this civilization variously had been Trojans, Christian Romans, Mongolians, and even Welshmen.

According to the Book of Mormon, the Indians were the remnants of a once-powerful nation which had ruled the entire American continent, and the mounds were the ruins of their highly developed civilization. Other contemporary accounts of Indian origins had recalled the Ten Lost Tribes of Israel, dispersed after the destruction of Jerusalem in about 600 B.C., to explain the presence of the Indians in the New World. Smith varied the story somewhat by following an eleventh group, which was an offshoot of Manasseh through Joseph. This tribe, warned of the forthcoming calamity, was guided by the Lord to America to people the as yet uninhabited continent. Pre-Columbian history, then, was really a continuation of Biblical history, and the newly discovered Book of Mormon was to be a more complete history of the Hebrew nation than was available in the Bible. (The history of the "New" World was actually pushed back even further than this, for Smith appended to his major narrative the brief story of the Jaredites, an even earlier group of settlers who had made their way to America from the Near East shortly after the building of the Tower of Babel but who had been exterminated in a great civil war. The account of the

Jaredites had also been written upon golden plates, which the new settlers had discovered.)

The American Israelites became a great civilization, built cities, "multiplied exceedingly, and spread upon the face of the land, and became exceedingly rich in gold, and in silver, and in precious things. . . ."[4] In a remarkable exegetical feat, Smith found evidence that the New World inhabitants had become Christians, thus providing for a "New Testament" in the Book of Mormon. John 10:16, where Jesus says, "and other sheep I have, which are not of this fold: them also must I bring, and they shall hear my voice; and there shall be one fold, and one shepherd," was interpreted as referring to the American Hebrews. This section of the Book of Mormon included an account of a postresurrection visit by Christ to the New World, where he performed miracles, preached, and set up a new church, ordaining twelve apostles to spread the gospel in America. "But despite or because of their good fortune [the American Hebrews] experience the same religious and political problems that the United States was experiencing in Smith's own time."[5] The Book of Mormon is replete with references to Jacksonian politics, the anti-Masonic furor of the late 1820s, and contemporary theological controversies; it champions free will and the efficacy of works, affirms that man is born unburdened with Adam's sin, and joins in the general enthusiasm for predicting the millennium.

Early in the narrative, the Hebrew colonists split into two factions, the Nephites and the Lamanites. The Nephites live righteously and prosper, but almost from the beginning the Lamanites are ungodly, and as punishment the Lord turns their skin dark reddish-brown. The Lamanites live in the wilderness and wage bow-and-arrow warfare against the civilized Nephites. "They are, in fact, the ancestors of the American Indians, although it is made clear that those Lamanites who return to the ways of virtue can recover the light skin of the Hebrew forefathers."[6] The Nephites also eventually become corrupt and the Lord decides to destroy them by means of fraternal warfare. Hence in the year 401 A.D. there is battle at the Hill Cumorah, and nearly all the Nephites are destroyed, leaving the American continent to the degenerate Lamanites. One remaining Nephite prophet, Mormon, records the story of his race on golden plates and gives them to his son, Moroni, who buries them atop Cumorah. These, then, were the plates uncovered by Joseph Smith.

The results of Smith's translation were published in 1830, in prose which borrowed much of its language and imagery from the King James Bible. The Church of Christ was founded on 6 April 1830 with an initial membership of six. The Book of Mormon, besides providing the church with its popular name, gave the new religion an aura of legitimacy—it was a revealed document, it provided a more complete

4. Book of Mormon, Jarom 8.

5. Curtis Dahl, "Mound Builders, Mormons, and William Cullen Bryant." *New England Quarterly* 34,2 (1961): 188.

6. Robert Silverberg, *Mound Builders of America* (New York, 1968), p. 93.

7. Ernest Lee Tuveson, *Redeemer Nation: The Idea of America's Millennial Role* (Chicago and London, 1968), p. 121, quoting from a poem written in 1804 by David Humphreys, "A Poem on the Future Glory of the United States."
8. Klaus J. Hansen, *Quest for Empire: The Political Kingdom of God and the Council of Fifty in Mormon History* (East Lansing, Mich., 1967), p. 30.

record of Old and New Testament history, and it attempted to explain and to demonstrate logically the connections among various religious and historical phenomena. Most important, the book provided the impetus for Smith and his followers to reestablish the native American church, the true church set up by Christ himself. The beliefs of the Latter-day Saints were in no way restricted to the Book of Mormon, however, even though at first it was the church's signal attraction. Having based his religion upon a manuscript whose location was revealed by the Lord and which was translated miraculously, Smith continued over the next few years to elaborate upon its doctrines by this same process of direct revelation from God to his modern-day prophet. These revelations are collectively known as the *Doctrine and Covenants* and contain 136 pronouncements received between 1828 and 1843 to help chart the course of the growing new religion.

Some of the most interesting of these revelations expanded the narrative of the Book of Mormon. They explained that after his expulsion from the Garden of Eden Adam had dwelt in "Adam-Ohndi-Ahman" in Daviess County, Missouri, near the town of Independence, which had itself been the actual site of the Garden. The rationale for this rearrangement of Biblical geography was that Noah had been carried by the flood from America to Palestine. The western hemisphere, not the Near East, was the source of all history and the birthplace of western civilization. Here Smith can be seen to share in the pervasive mystique of the American continent as a new Eden, which the discovery of America had stimulated. This wild new continent, unsullied by dissolute civilizations and corrupted religions, could be the place where man might achieve both material progress and spiritual rebirth. For nineteenth-century Americans this belief was also related to dreams of a continental empire as well as to millennial hopes. America was to "blossom as the rose, Like Salem flourish and like Eden bloom."[7] This new Eden, stretching from Atlantic to Pacific, was to regenerate the world and was to be the epicenter of an upheaval which would spread over all the earth.

This quest for an earthly paradise was a driving force in Mormon life. Indeed, the location of this future paradise was concrete and specific, unlike the generalizations of those for whom the whole continent was to become utopia. "The historical vision of Joseph Smith . . . made it possible to conjure from the bones of an American Adam and his pre-Columbian descendants an image of America that could motivate those who believed in this past to recreate the Garden of Eden in its original setting. It was no accident that the Mormons dreamed of building the new Jerusalem in the vicinity of the location where Adam had presumably dwelt."[8] In 1830 Smith declared that Zion was to be located on land bordering that of the Lamanites (the American Indians), which at that time was in western Missouri.

The Edenic myth was an important concept, for the Mormons believed literally in the "gathering of Israel." This, of course, is a recurrent Old Testament theme, which anticipates regeneration of the Hebrew nation at an unspecified future time. The gathering will bring together in Zion the people of Israel who were dispersed into captivity first by the Assyrians and then by Nebuchadnezzar, who put a definitive end to Jewish civilization by capturing Jerusalem and desecrating the temple. As foretold in Isaiah 12:11–21:

> And it shall come to pass in that day, that the Lord shall set his hand again the second time to recover the remnant of his people, which shall be left, from Assyria, and from Egypt . . . and from Shinar, and from the islands of the sea.
> And he shall set up an ensign for the nations, and shall assemble the outcasts of Israel, and gather together the dispersed of Judah from the four corners of the earth.

The gathering of all people to Zion was a necessary first step for establishing the millennial kingdom, and Joseph Smith proposed that the time for its achievement was at hand.

The instrument which would bring this about was of course the new church. The Catholic church, referred to in the Book of Mormon as "the great and abominable church of all the earth," and all Protestant denominations were repudiated as having lost the apostolic succession of Christ. In the eyes of Smith and his followers, the true church and legitimate priesthood of God had been withdrawn from the earth shortly after the death of the apostles. (Interestingly, the battle at the Hill Cumorah was dated 401 A.D., about the time that Protestant millennialists believed the Christian church had been taken over by the Antichrist, in the person of the Pope.) The Prophet, as he was known to the faithful, "restored" the true church not by interpretation of the Bible, which he believed had been adulterated through faulty translation, but by the direct action of the Lord, thus bypassing sectarian and denominational controversies. The authority to baptize was conferred upon Smith in 1829 by John the Baptist, who appeared to Smith and his secretary, Oliver Cowdery, in a vision.

In 1830 a second priesthood was restored by Peter, James, and John, i.e., the Melchizedek, the highest authority in the church. It was to this priesthood that the president of the church belonged, and its function was to "administer in spiritual things," as the revelation stated. By means of such revelations, the entire framework of the infant sect was laid out, purportedly restoring Christianity to its original and pristine state prior to the Lord's having taken away the condition of grace from the earth. Within the two priesthoods, the Aaronic and the Melchizedek, there were twelve apostles, a Council of Seventy, deacons, priests, bishops, teachers, and elders, all with special duties. The Prophet (Smith was also president of the church) asserted that this was the same organization as that set up by Christ himself during his ministry in the New World and claimed for it the same spiritual authority.

Inherent in the notion of the gathering was the necessity of the Latter-day Saints'[9] physically removing themselves from the rest of society. In so doing, the Saints were following a typical sectarian pattern of the withdrawal of the elect from secular life. But unlike many other sects, Smith actively worked to attract people to his camp, for the gathering was eventually to encompass all of the world's population. In 1831 Smith moved with his followers to Kirtland, Ohio, where he had managed to convert the entire congregation of Disciples of Christ (Campbellites) and their leader, Sidney Rigdon, to Mormonism. From there he sent out a call to the remaining Saints in the east to remove themselves to Kirtland. Others were attracted by rumors of a great new prophet and his gospel and by reports of miraculous healings. By 1833 Kirtland was a Mormon town, numbering about a thousand. Operating under a system known as the United Order of Enoch, members of the colony deeded all their property to the church and were given back what land and goods they needed. In this experimentation with communistic economics they resembled other religious and secular societies of the time.

Mormonism at Kirtland, where its first temple was raised, was still a simple and rather typical frontier faith. Some of its most basic and distinctive theology was yet to be developed. There were at this time no elaborate rituals, traditional marital relationships were maintained, and Smith in fact suppressed some of the more extravagant practices like speaking in tongues. With its early-Christian type of organization, charismatic leader, emphasis on revelation and visions, revival-style meetings, and millennial aspirations, Mormonism's distinction was its possession of a written testament.

Chapter 2

Latter-day Temples

Early Mormonism combined and articulated a variety of interests prevalent in the 1820s and 1830s. What makes it so unusual is that it was one of very few early nineteenth-century popular sects to survive the era which had produced it. Mormonism not only endured persecution by its neighbors, the murder of its prophet, and the long trek across the plains to the Great Salt Lake, but has been able to negotiate the transition from the nineteenth to the twentieth century. Mormonism is also the only one of these sects to have fashioned a monumental religious architecture. It produced an architectural form unique to itself, the temple, and created a style sufficiently different from other revival styles of the nineteenth century to be recognizable as purely Mormon.

Though democratic in origin, since it did not derive sanction from an entrenched ecclesiastical organization, Mormonism very quickly became an authoritarian religion. The church offices set up by Smith's revelations maintained a strict hierarchy, with definite requirements for progressing from one level to the next. Though all church members were incorporated into the bureaucratic structure, decisions in temporal matters were made by Smith and his council of high priests. Doctrinal matters were pronounced upon by the prophet alone, and since his authority was God-given, it was not subject to question.

Temple-building was, and is, very much a product of the authoritarian nature of the Mormon church. The impetus for building a temple came not from the people, even though Mormons today regard their early temples as manifestations of steadfast faith and devotion to an ideal. Latter-day Saint temples have always been the domain of the president of the church, a tradition instituted by Joseph Smith at Kirtland. The decision to build a temple, selection of the site, allocation of labor and community resources to construct it, and the employment of architects were all undertaken by the president and sustained by a vote of the assembled membership. Officially the form which the structure took was ascertained by direct revelation. The contribution of the people was in the physical labor and financial support required to actually put the building up, an impressive contribution indeed considering the limited resources of the Saints and the challenging conditions prevailing in Ohio, Illinois, and Utah. Temples are still built in much the same way today, though architectural specifications are no longer given through revelation. (The president does, however, receive an initial revelation that a new temple is needed.) The church now maintains its own architectural office in Salt Lake City, staffed by Mormons, where plans for temples and other church buildings are produced. Temples are financed by voluntary contributions above and beyond the tithe which all Mormons pay.

Mormon temples are used today for the performance of secret ritual, to be discussed in later chapters. Some meetings of high officials are held in the temples, but this is a subsidiary function of the buildings. Temple ritual is a prerequisite for partaking of the joys of the afterlife, for it is only in a temple that certain necessary blessings can be received. The ritual is supplementary to regular worship services, which do not in any way resemble what goes on in the temple. Weekly services are held in ward chapels, which one attends according to place of residence, or ward, and are comparable to a very simple Protestant service. The temple is thus not synonymous with the church, for it is not a meetinghouse. The present-day concept of the Mormon temple is based upon the Solomonic idea of the temple as Holy of Holies, a sacred structure reserved for the performance of sanctified ceremony by an elect group. After the dedication of a temple, it is closed to all non-Mormons (gentiles), and even members of the church must be in good standing to go through. A visit to a temple must be arranged in advance, and the participant must present a written recommendation from his bishop before being allowed to enter.

Since 1833 the Latter-day Saints have completed eighteen temples in the United States, Europe, and New Zealand. Six were finished in the nineteenth century. The first of these was built at Kirtland, 1833–1836, and the second, at Nauvoo, Illinois, was barely completed when the Saints were forced to abandon it and their city in 1846. The Nauvoo temple was demolished by a tornado in 1850, an event which the Mormons have interpreted as divine intervention to prevent the use of a sacred structure for profane purposes. The remaining four nineteenth-century temples are in Utah, at Salt Lake City, 1853–1893, St. George, 1871–1877, Logan, 1877–1884, and Manti, 1877–1888 (figure 1).

The consideration of these six temples as a group is determined by more than their existence within the confines of a single century. A consistent stylistic development is apparent from Kirtland and Nauvoo to Salt Lake City, which served as the prototype for the other Utah temples even though it was the last to be completed. The Utah temples are generically related and can be seen as the culmination of an attempt to represent visually, through architecture, a new and unique theology. All the Utah temples are constructed of massive, thick-walled masonry, in a variant of the castellated Gothic style. The but-

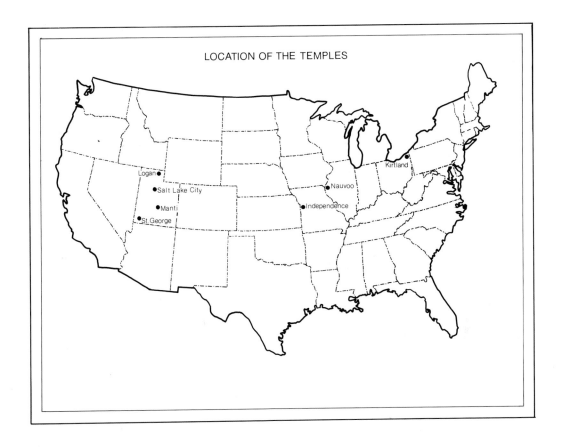

1. Location of the temple sites

tresses, crenellations, and other medieval elements are totally non-functional, serving only as decoration for the simple, rectangular body of the building. The structures relate in shape and proportions to the earlier temples at Nauvoo and Kirtland. With the exception of St. George they are double-ended, each end having three towers of unequal height whose styles are not necessarily consistent with that of the temple body proper. A salient feature of all is the inclusion of two doors on either one or both facades. From the exterior these temples convey the impression of having two stories articulated by rows of high, round-arched windows. At Salt Lake City and St. George these alternate with two rows of elliptical or round windows, creating a less harmonious elevation than the simplified version employed at Logan and Manti. In actuality the two-story division is a retention of the form established at Kirtland and does not necessarily correspond to the internal arrangement of these later structures. Logan, for example, though ostensibly having two main floors, contains five levels. Nauvoo and all the Utah temples have a deep basement containing a large baptismal font and rooms for preparation for the ceremonies, which are lighted from above by the basement windows. The remaining stories contain ritual rooms of varying sizes, meeting rooms, and offices for temple functionaries. In addition there is in one of the upper stories of each temple in Utah a large room used for special convocations.

As the exterior elevation does not markedly reflect the interior disposition of rooms, so the decoration of the interior bears no consistent relationship to the style of the architecture. Some ritual rooms contain landscape murals by local Mormon artists referring in subject to the purpose of the room, while the remainder indulge in highly ornate Second Empire plushness (figure 2). Extensive consideration of the interior ornamentation would be an impracticable project for a non-Mormon, since absolutely no exceptions are made to the policy of excluding all but accredited participants in the ceremonies. Nonetheless, a clear understanding of the meaning of Mormon architecture can be gained without actually going into the temples. Decoration and interior disposition of the rooms will be considered where they have bearing upon the interpretation of the buildings in general. The impression to be gained from photographs which are available is that the interior is meant to contrast with the fortified severity of the face which the temples present to the outside world. Once he has passed through the portals of the temple, the true believer is made aware through magnificence of materials that he has entered the sanctified, otherworldly realm of the Lord, an earthly equivalent of the paradise to which the proper performance of the temple rites will lead.

Following the completion of the Salt Lake City temple in 1893, there was a pause in construction of these buildings until 1915, when the temple at Laie, Oahu, Hawaii was begun (figure 3). This first temple of

2. Celestial Room, Salt Lake temple

3. *Hawaii temple*

4. Los Angeles temple

5. *Provo temple*

6. *Washington, D.C. temple*

7. *Ward chapel, St. George, Utah*

8. *St. George tabernacle*

9. Coalville, Utah, tabernacle

10. Ward chapel, Parowan, Utah

the twentieth century departed from the Utah style dramatically. The castellated Gothic disappeared entirely, to be replaced by a more contemporary mode echoing Frank Lloyd Wright's architecture, especially his Unity Temple. Even the distinctive double-ended form was rejected, along with the multiple towers, in favor of a centralized Greek cross plan that seems to refer to the temples of the Central American Indians, which Latter-day Saints believe to be the artifacts of the civilization chronicled in the Book of Mormon. The succeeding temples have drifted aimlessly to an astylistic "modern" conglomeration of abstract shapes and geometric decoration, as in the Los Angeles temple, 1951–1956 (figure 4). Though the interior purposes of the newer temples are the same as those of the temples in the Utah style, no particular form is associated with the temple in the twentieth century—some are centralized, some longitudinal, and two of the most recent, at Ogden and at Provo, Utah (figure 5) are oval, elevated upon a square base. In something of a departure from this situation, the newly completed temple at Washington, D.C. has even turned to quoting its own past tradition and is a streamlined interpretation of the temple in Salt Lake City (figure 6).

The relatively innocuous style of the modern temples is applied with equal ease to the temple and to the much lesser and—more importantly—functionally different structures, the ward chapels (figure 7). This is in contrast to the building practice of the Mormons in the nineteenth century. No nineteenth-century chapels were built in the castellated style, nor were any tabernacles (large assembly halls for meetings of "stakes"—territorial groupings of several wards). Though the tabernacles might at times incorporate certain elements seen on the temples, they were never combined in such a way as to be mistaken for a temple. For example, the St. George tabernacle, 1871–1877 (figure 8), has two doors, but in form it is essentially a colonial meetinghouse embellished with Greek Revival entablatures and Victorian brackets. The Coalville tabernacle, begun in 1879 (figure 9), was, before being razed in 1971, a cruciform-plan, eclectic Second Empire Gothic building with magnificently exaggerated buttresses and finials. Parowan ward chapel (figure 10) with its double doors is typical in its simplicity of the smaller chapels found throughout Utah. In building the tabernacles there seems to have been considerable freedom in matters of style and form, and it is only the temples which manifested a unity of concept.

The problem of nineteenth-century Mormon temple architecture, then, concerns the creation of the Utah style and the reasons for its development, since there evidently was choice involved and not just random selection and an arbitrary combination of elements. Other questions to be examined are the relationship of Mormon temple architecture to other types of American buildings, the possible influences of this other architecture upon the creation of a Mormon style, and, above all, what the temples meant to the Latter-day Saints in the nineteenth century. Although the temples were ostensibly dependent on the Lord for the form they took, since plans were provided by revelation, consideration must be given to the part which the official church architects played in their design and construction, for both Smith and his successor, Brigham Young, employed an architect or architects for all the temples. Finally it must be determined why the nineteenth-century style was abandoned.

There has been no study of temple architecture by non-Mormons, perhaps because Utah even today remains a relatively isolated part of the United States, especially those areas in which the temples outside Salt Lake City are located. Only a few fragments are left of the temple at Nauvoo, and Kirtland is located in a dingy suburb of Cleveland. In addition to inconvenient location and the destruction of the most impressive eastern example, the temples, like many Victorian buildings, have not been deemed worthy of study for their architectural merits. By their contemporaries the Mormon temples were either totally ignored or regarded with a mixture of amusement and contempt. The *American Architect and Building News* reported in 1878:

> It is said that the walls of the Mormon Temple at Salt Lake City are now eighteen feet above the surface of the ground. Work was begun twenty-four years ago, and if the same rate of progress is preserved throughout, the walls, which are to be 120 feet high, will be finished in about 150 years.

The only other mention of the Mormons in a professional architectural magazine occurred in a report on the bathroom fixtures exhibited at the World's Columbian Exposition of 1893:

> The Standard Manufacturing Company also show what is said to be the largest bath-tub ever made. It is a replica of a dozen made for the Mormon temple at Salt Lake City, and is 10 or 12 feet long and proportionately deep. Unfortunately no information as to the nature of the religious ceremony in which these 12 monster bath-tubs figure is given.[1]

Mormonism at this time was still a mysterious sect, and it is understandable that the sophisticated east paid no attention to these provincial buildings whose architects were not members of the professional community.

Even today, virtually no one has studied the temples. John Maas does include a photograph of the Manti temple in his book *The Gingerbread Age*, but Gowans, in *Images of American Living*, regards the Salt Lake City temple as only a quaint aberration of eclectic nineteenth-century revivalism. Speaking of the eccentricities of many who decided to build in the Gothic style, he says:

1. Barr Ferree, "Architecture," *Engineering Magazine* 6, 1 (1893): 100. The tubs were installed in the basement of the Salt Lake City temple and are used in the baptismal ceremony.

2. Alan Gowans,
*Images of American
Living* (New York
and Philadelphia,
1964), p. 306.
3. Hugh W. Nibley,
in the *Millennial
Star* 120, 8 (1958):
247.
4. James E. Tal-
mage, *The House of
the Lord* (Salt Lake
City, 1968), p. 144.

Or you heard how the Mormons—they of the gold plates and the many wives—after earlier essays in vaguely Romanesque-cum-Masonic temple designs, had finally settled on an enormous Gothic-pinnacled temple at Salt Lake as the perfect expression of their Church of Jesus Christ of Latter-day Saints.[2]

Only recently, with the growing interest in nineteenth-century vernacular architecture, has serious consideration been accorded the temples. The Historic American Buildings Survey has published a catalogue for the state of Utah in which the temples, as well as other examples of Mormon architecture, are briefly discussed.

The Mormons themselves have never been concerned with questions of architectural theory, and there are no writings pertaining to style by any of the men involved in the planning of the temples. Today's Latter-day Saints admire their temples primarily for the effort expended by a struggling pioneer population to build monuments to their God and to their religion. The viewpoint is historical, not critical. Mormon evaluation of the temples is, of course, strongly influenced by the belief that they are sacred structures built on God-given plan. Mormon writing discusses, besides factual data, the importance of the buildings in the Mormon eschatological system and recognizes their holiness and the consequent need to revere them. This emotional and spiritual attachment to the temples has thus far precluded dispassionate architectural criticism and has led to such extravagant statements as the following, made by a professor of religious history at Brigham Young University, the church college:

> ... in establishing their temples the Mormons did not adopt traditional forms: with them the temple and its rites are absolutely pristine. In contrast the church and temple architecture of the world is an exotic jumble, a bewildering complex of borrowed motifs, a persistent effort to work back through the centuries to some golden time and place when men still had the light.[3]

At a time when Mormonism was conscientiously attempting to become a thoroughly acceptable religion, Talmage, the foremost writer on the temples, commented:

> As to architectural design the Temple belongs to a class of its own. Originality rather than novelty characterizes every prominent feature. And yet there is nothing apparent that speaks of strained effort for departure from more conventional lines. The Temple is no oddity in architecture; on the contrary, it is strictly in place both as to material environment and spiritual atmosphere.[4]

These statements do not, however, explain why the temples look the way they do. The Utah temples have meaning beyond their reference to steadfastness and devotion—meaning which is inseparable with specific internal and external factors in Mormon history. Mormonism has changed since the nineteenth century. Once an isolationist utopian sect, it is now a conservative, established religion. It can be surmised, therefore, that the temples signify something different today from what they did when they were built. The assumption can also be made that since the Mormons did not embrace conventional Christian theology, normative Christian architectural forms and symbols necessarily underwent some transformation or were entirely supplanted by those having more appropriate associations for the Latter-day Saints. The four Utah temples are the end result of an architectural development which reflects changes in the doctrine, ritual, and politics of the Mormon church. As its theology became more complex and its worship more highly ritualized, the temples changed from the simple and quite primitive architecture of the Kirtland temple to an architectural style expressive of the peculiar and isolated situation of Mormon civilization in the Great Salt Lake valley. They are, in fact, tangible expressions of what became in Salt Lake City a virtual theocracy, whose stated goal was the establishment of God's kingdom on earth. It is in Utah that the American dream of the restoration of Eden climaxes with an attempt to fulfill Isaiah's prophecy literally, and the four Utah temples are the only American architecture to give substantive form to this dream.

Chapter 3

Temple-Building Begins

In 1833, only three years after the formal organization of the church, the Mormons began to build a temple at Kirtland. Their first architectural planning, however, preceded the Kirtland effort by two years. Joseph Smith had always regarded Kirtland as only a temporary gathering place for the Saints. The permanent location of their settlement was to be on what was then the western frontier, where there was more land available and fewer people to hamper the expansion of the Mormon settlement, for even in 1830 Ohio was rapidly filling up as people streamed in from the east. Smith thus sent out an advance force to buy land and begin the establishment of a colony in western Missouri, in anticipation of moving the Kirtland group to what he had designated as the land of Zion, consecrated by the Lord for the gathering of the Saints. On a visit to Missouri in July 1831, he selected the site for the temple, not far from the courthouse in Independence, and in August Smith dedicated the ground which was to be used.

As Independence had been the site of the Garden of Eden, to erect a temple there was an essential first step in the building up of the earthly paradise. It was to the temple that all nations would be gathered in those last days preceding the Lord's coming, and Smith had said in a revelation that Christ would come to his temple. This explains why such an undertaking was considered even before a substantial settlement was founded. It was needed as a locus for the gathering as well as serving as a house of worship, and simply setting aside a plot of ground consecrated for the construction of a temple was an incentive for those already living at Kirtland to move to a considerably less civilized part of the country.

Calling the projected structure a temple rather than a church emphasized the continuity between Latter-day Saints and the Hebrews, not only the Hebrews of Palestine, but the Nephites of the Book of Mormon, who had built a temple on the American continent patterned after the Temple of Solomon:

> And I, Nephi, did build a temple; and I did construct it after the manner of the temple of Solomon save it were not built of so many

1. Book of Mormon, II Nephi 5:16. This is the only description of the New World temple offered in the Book of Mormon. Besides this passage, the temple is mentioned only a few times, once, interestingly, as the place of the appearance of the risen Christ to the Nephites.
2. Joseph Smith, *History of the Church*, I, p. 358.
3. Revelation 21:16.
4. Smith, *History of the Church*, I, p. 358.

precious things; for they were not to be found upon the land. . . . But the manner of construction was like unto the temple of Solomon; and the workmanship thereof was exceeding fine.[1]

The temple at Independence was thus to be a replacement for this as well as a modern-day equivalent of the Solomonic structure, at least insofar as it was sanctified by the Lord, not by men. By not designating his building a church, Smith also escaped association with the Protestant denominations which he had repudiated. The Mormons' temple was not to be one of many religious buildings competing for worshippers of a corrupted faith, but unique to the newly restored religion.

In June 1833 Smith sent to the outpost in Missouri a plat of the city of Zion which he wanted built at Independence. Zion, according to Mormon doctrine, was both a land and a city, the city identified by Smith with the New Jerusalem, religious capital of the western hemisphere (figure 11). The city was to be a grid one mile on each side, with lots of equal size, broad streets, and a brick house on each lot. Surrounding it would be an extensive agricultural area kept separate from the civic and residential nucleus. Zion was planned not merely as an isolated religious community, but as the eventual center of an expanding agrarian empire, for "when this square is thus laid up and supplied, lay off another in the same way, and so fill up the world in the last days; and let every man live in the city for this is the city of Zion."[2] Here was to be the millennial kingdom, an orderly utopia of righteousness and prosperity, not unlike Robert Owen's communitarian experiments in its desire for self-sufficiency, and similar in layout to the Rappites' town of Harmony, Pennsylvania.

The origin of a square city set in the middle of agricultural land was probably Biblical, for such an arrangement is mentioned by Ezekiel and in Numbers and Leviticus. John's vision of the heavenly city is of one which "lieth foursquare, and the length is as large as the breadth."[3] The center of Zion was to be set aside for special use:

> The painted squares in the middle are for public buildings. The one without any figures is for storehouses for the Bishop, and to be devoted to his use. Figure first is for temples for the use of the Presidency, the circles inside of the squares, are the places for the temples. You will see it contains twelve figures, two are for the temples of the lesser Priesthood. It is also to contain twelve temples.
>
> The whole plot is supposed to contain from fifteen to twenty thousand people; you will therefore see that it will require twenty-four buildings to supply them with houses of worship, schools, etc., and none of these temples are to be smaller than the one of which we send you a draft. . . .[4]

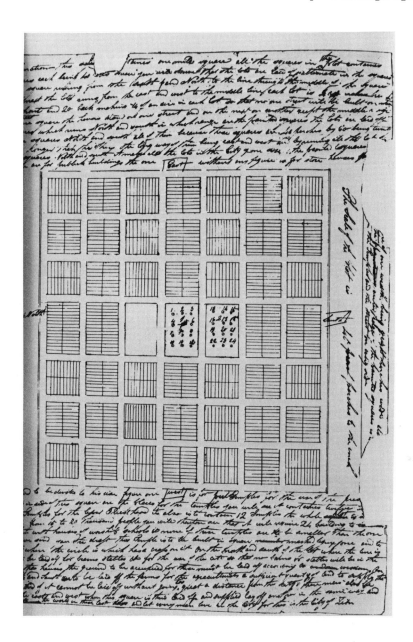

11. Joseph Smith's plat of Zion

Smith seems to have been referring to the temples synonymously with civic buildings, and they evidently were to combine several functions, serving as schools besides being houses of worship. It is not clear whether they were envisioned as some sort of community hall, to be put to whatever civic or religious function was called for, or whether each was to have its own specific purpose in this extravagantly imagined future city.

Ezekiel may have been the derivation of the cluster of temples in the middle of the city, but the number, twenty-four, which Smith planned, was based upon the various offices within the two Mormon priesthoods. Each of the three levels in either priesthood was assigned a group of three temples for its superintendency.[5] The remaining two groups of three temples were allotted to the presidency (Smith and his two counselors) and the bishop and his two counselors. The first temple to be commenced was for the presidency, and in all likelihood Smith had no concrete plans beyond a first temple at this time.

The temple at Independence was never built, due to the hostility of the Missourians, whose resentment of the Mormon influx eventually reached such a pitch that the Saints were forcibly expelled, first from Jackson County, in 1833, and finally, in 1838, from Missouri altogether. There remain, however, two sets of drawings for this temple, now in the Church of Jesus Christ of Latter-day Saints Church Historian's Office in Salt Lake City. These were given to the church in 1865 by the widow of Bishop Edward Partridge, who had been in charge of the Mormon communities in Missouri. At the time the drawings were presented the donor indicated that they had been intended as plans for the Independence temple and had been sent to Missouri by Joseph Smith in either 1832 or 1833. The specifications on one set of drawings correspond in almost every detail to the written description of the "House of the Lord to be erected in Zion" which Smith had entered in his journal under the date 25 June 1833 along with the details of the plat. These are the only significant drawings of the Independence temple, and since they are so similar to the temple actually built at Kirtland, they should be regarded as the first step in the development of ideas about the building in Ohio. Preparations were being made for erecting a temple at Kirtland in the beginning of June 1833, so it is quite likely that plans for both Independence and Kirtland were drawn up at the same time. As conditions worsened in Missouri, Smith decided to abandon any immediate hopes for a temple in Zion and turned his efforts to Kirtland, where there was relative security and stability. To explain why a temple was being built at a location other than the final destination, Smith likened the church to a giant tent whose center was Zion, with other Mormon towns as "stakes" of the metaphorical tent, subsidiary to the center post but lending support and embraced by the widespread cover. Kirtland was such a stake, and its temple was to be one of many built by the Saints, though Independence was, and still is, regarded as the place where the greatest of all temples will be constructed.

6. Smith, *History of the Church*, I, p. 361.

The drawings for the Independence temple are by two different hands. One set, consisting of a floor plan, facade, and side elevation, evidently represents the original concept, since the drawing is sketchily done in freehand and lacks details. These are not signed and the handwriting has not been identified. The second set—ground plan, side elevation, east and west facades—is more precisely drawn, and the drawing of the east end (figure 12) bears the signature of Frederick G. Williams, a member of the first presidency (Smith, Williams, and Sidney Rigdon) at Kirtland. Both sets are essentially the same, though Williams's drawings increase the number of windows on the flanks from five to nine, the length from eighty-seven to ninety-seven feet, and include a few more details. Both contain handwritten instructions explaining the drawings and giving general directions for the construction of the building, again with only minor changes in the Williams set. The instructions on the first set are those found in Joseph Smith's *History of the Church*.

Made of brick and stone like the houses in the city of Zion, the temple was to have been simple, but solidly built. Its profile would have been long and low, for while the width was specified as sixty-one feet, the total height of the two stories, excluding the pediment, was given as only twenty-eight feet. This primitive, shed-like structure is really an example of early Mormon building rather than architecture, for its appearance seems to have been dictated exclusively by functional needs with no concern for style, harmony of proportion, or satisfactory interrelationship of parts.

Each of the two stories of the temple was to have a meeting room with an elliptically arched ceiling. Two aisles would separate the blocks of pews from each other, and at either end of each hall there was to be a set of tiered pulpits for those officiating in the services. Four fireplaces, one near each corner, would provide heat for the rooms. There are no details given about interior ornamentation—what concerned Smith most were the dimensions and arrangement of the interior halls and the necessity of finishing the building with the best materials available, as is seen in his remarks about the pulpits and windows:

> The pulpits are to be finished with panel work, in the best workmanlike manner; and the building to be constructed of stone and brick of the best quality. . . . The windows are to have each forty-eight lights, of seven by nine glass, six one way and eight the other; the sides and lintels of the windows to be of hewn stone. . . .[6]

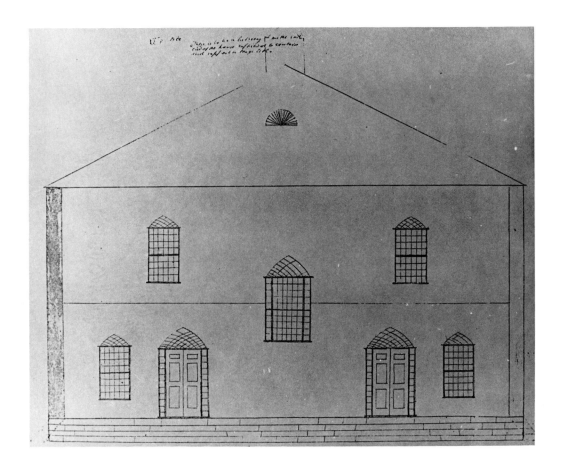

12. *Williams's drawing of the Independence temple*

7. *Ibid.*

The drawings must have been intended to serve primarily as a guide to the local builders at Independence, giving them necessary directions, but leaving many of the details to be worked out by those doing the construction.

In the instructions which accompanied these drawings, the structure was consistently referred to as either the "House of the Lord" or simple as a "house." As it appears in the drawings, the temple did seem to be essentially an overgrown domestic structure possessing few features associated with a church—perhaps purposely. The temple was to have been a plain, pedimented building, with only the Gothic windows indicating any interest in stylistic ornamentation, and with a belfry included in the Williams drawings. It was to have been distinguished from the houses around it primarily by the wide space surrounding it and by height. "Let the foundation of the house be of stone; let it be raised sufficiently high to allow of banking up so high as to admit of a descent every way from the house, so far as to divide the distance between this house, and the one next to it." [7]

A further reason for the appellation "house," beyond the ordinary metaphor of the church or temple as house of the Lord, is found in the Bible. In the revelations about Kirtland and Independence, the interior of the building is always called the "inner court," terminology patently derived from Biblical descriptions of Solomon's Temple, especially those found in I Kings, as is the use of the word "house" to mean "temple." Smith was evidently trying to give his building legitimacy by verbally linking it with the Biblical temple, emphasizing that this was to be a temple in the truest sense, befitting a religion which claimed to have reestablished the Hebrews' line of succession. (It should be remembered, too, that it was really the Lord who was the author of the revelations about the temples, and he would of course speak of them in the same way as he had in Solomon's day.) In all other respects, though, the temple was to have been an uncomplicated, serviceable hall, typical of sectarian or communitarian architecture such as that seen in Shaker communities, and suitable to the needs of the rude frontier settlement which existed in Missouri at the time.

The Prophet began to give serious thought to the temple at Kirtland in the spring of 1833. The revelation giving the dimensions was received in May, but evidently nothing was done, for in June the Lord was moved to chastise the people of Kirtland for dragging their feet in this matter. Following the rebuke, work was begun in earnest, with the first load of stone being hauled to the site on 5 June. As the town had already been settled before the arrival of the Mormons, the temple did not form the center of a master plat as it would have at Zion. There are no written instructions comparable to those given for the Independence temple, no plans, and little mention of it in revelations or in Smith's *History of the Church*, the published version of the church founder's journal. Strictly speaking, there was no single architect of

8. Orson Pratt, in *Journal of Discourses*, XIV, p. 273.
9. Smith, *History of the Church*, I, p. 352.
10. Truman O. Angell to John Taylor and Counsel, 11 March, 1885, letter in the Church Historian's Office, Church of Jesus Christ of Latter-day Saints, Salt Lake City.

the building, though credit must undoubtedly be given to Joseph Smith for the general arrangement of the interior and probably the basic ideas of the elevation. Since this was ostensibly a building whose plan was revealed by God, it would have been self-contradictory for Smith to have recorded which men were responsible for particular aspects of the building, or what its sources were. For all practical purposes it *was* a revealed plan, since this is the only answer which contemporary sources provide:

> When the Lord commanded this people to build a house in the land of Kirtland, he gave them the pattern by vision from heaven, and commanded them to build that house according to the heavenly pattern that he by his voice had inspired to his servants.[8]

The relationship of the temple to contemporary or earlier architecture can be ascertained only through evidence provided by the appearance of the building itself.

Smith had had no experience in the building trade, and at this early date there were few among the Mormons who had. Some slight indication of how the temple must have been planned is hinted at in the revelation, where the Lord says, ". . . let the house be built, not after the manner of the world; for I give not unto you that ye shall live after the manner of the world; Therefore, let it be built after the manner which I shall show unto three of you, whom ye shall appoint and ordain unto this power." A few days later, Smith, Sidney Rigdon, and Frederick G. Williams were appointed by a conference of high priests to "obtain a draft or construction"[9] of the temple. Truman Angell, who later became the official church architect in Salt Lake City, also recalled that Rigdon and Williams were involved in designing the temple. Writing in 1885, he said:

> I did not go to Kirtland until the fall of 1835. At this time I went to work upon the Kirtland Temple. . . . F. G. Williams came into the Temple about the time the main hall first floor was ready for dedication. He was asked, how does the house look to you. He answered that it looked to him like the model he had seen.
>
> He said President Joseph, Sidney Rigdon and himself were called to come before the Lord and the model was shown to them.
>
> He said the vision of the Temple was thus shown them and he could not see the difference between it and the House as built.[10]

Before joining the Saints, Rigdon had been a Campbellite preacher and Williams, a resident of Connecticut, had been a physician before being converted to Mormonism by missionaries. These three architectural neophytes must have gotten together to work out, through a process of intuition, the general ideas to supplement Smith's original revelation, then enlisted anyone who had had any experience to help them. Williams had produced the more precise of the two sets of drawings for Independence and may also have been the draftsman for Kirtland, though it is not known how far his participation extended.

The master builder was sought from outside the Kirtland community. Artemus Millett, a builder of bridges and culverts for the British government in Canada, recorded that he was baptized into the church by Brigham Young in 1833:

> . . . Brigham Young announced that he had a mission for me. The Prophet Joseph wanted me to go to Kirtland Ohio and take charge of the mason work on the Temple as they were going to build a Temple there. So I closed out my business there and in April 1834 I moved to Kirtland . . . and I did have full superintendency of the building. . . .[11]

Millett selected stone and employed assistants to help with the plastering and carpentry, though since he did not arrive in Kirtland until 1834, he could not have had anything to do with the original conception of the structure. One Jacob Bump of Silver Creek, New York, took charge of the plastering of the interior, and it is known that Brigham Young, who had been a carpenter, joiner, painter, and glazier, had something to do with the painting of the inside. It is impossible to determine who was responsible for the various parts of the building, but ultimately this is not of great import, since the details can all be found in commonly used builders' guides.

The Kirtland temple was completed in 1836 and has had no major alterations since that time, though some damage was incurred after the Saints abandoned it in 1838. It was used briefly as a stable and then as a public school for some forty years, but the interior woodwork is intact. The temple has been restored by the Reorganized Church of Jesus Christ of Latter Day Saints, based in Independence, to whom it was awarded by legal decision in 1880. Unlike the temples of Utah, the Kirtland temple is open to the public, for the Reorganized Church has no secret ritual and uses the temple, the only one belonging to this group, for worship services on special occasions.

When first finished, and before the encroaching Cleveland suburbs hemmed it in, the temple must have presented a striking spectacle to the inhabitants of the small communities in northeastern Ohio. The site is the highest in the area, overlooking the East Chagrin valley, and from the tower it is possible to see Lake Erie, six miles away. The dimensions are also fairly impressive, for from basement to tower the height is approximately 110 feet. The plan was to construct the temple of brick, and for this purpose the church bought a plot of land adjoining the temple site where a clay deposit and brick kiln were located. However the kiln was found to be defective and the building medium was changed to roughly cut local sandstone, two feet thick, covered with plaster. The original plaster was most unusual for this part of the country, for it was made up of crushed glassware donated by the

11. Biography of Artemus Millett, manuscript in the Church Historian's Office, Salt Lake City.

12. Nathaniel
Hawthorne, *The
Scarlet Letter*, in-
troduction by Edwin
H. Cady (Colum-
bus, 1969), p. 103.
13. Henry Howe,
*Historical Collec-
tions of Ohio* (Cin-
cinnati, 1851), p.
282.
14. Alan Gowans,
*Images of American
Living* (New York
and Philadelphia,
1964), p. 218.

women of the town. This made the entire building sparkle when the
sunlight struck the walls and must have presented an appearance like
that of Governor Bellingham's mansion in Hawthorne's *The Scarlet
Letter*:

> It had indeed a very cheery aspect; the walls being overspread
> with a kind of stucco, in which fragments of broken glass were
> plentifully intermixed; so that, when the sunshine fell aslantwise
> over the front of the edifice, it glittered and sparkled as if
> diamonds had been flung against it by the double handful.[12]

This stucco was a variation of a very old building technique known
as rough cast, a method for achieving a textured wall surface by mix-
ing extraneous material, usually pebbles, into plaster. Though it was
widely used in England, in America its use was confined to New England, where it was employed in a limited way during the colonial
period. Its appearance at Kirtland in the 1830s was extremely anach-
ronistic. Henry Howe, who traveled through Ohio in the 1840s, reported that the plaster of the temple was a faded blue,[13] and the desired effect of masonry construction was achieved by tracing lines on
the plaster to simulate bricks (figure 13).

The general disposition of exterior elements (figure 14) is closely
related to the plans for the Independence temple. The greatest dis-
similarities are the inclusion of more ornament and the proportions.
The Kirtland temple has lost the peculiarly shed-like dimensions of the
Independence drawings—it is shorter, narrower, and higher, and looks
more "religious." Its proportions are those of a church of the federal
era, and its details are provincial and severely reduced adaptations of
the federal-Georgian vocabulary. It is apparent that the unusual qualities the temple possesses are due not to the architectural motifs themselves, which are all part of the standard usage of the building trade,
but to the unorthodox way in which they were arranged. The Kirtland
temple is an excellent example of the architecture of the western and
northern frontiers belonging to the two or three decades after the Revolutionary War, an architecture which "can rarely be judged in terms
of any systematic scheme of classical evolution."[14] Post-Revolutionary
architecture of this type is characterized by eclectic borrowing of stylistic motifs and the retention of forms which were outmoded in more
progressive areas of the country. It often represents an expression of
the rural classes, an appropriate categorization of the Mormon population of the early nineteenth century.

The town of Kirtland was located directly on the emigration route
which started in the Berkshires and moved westward through the
Burned-over District into Ohio and other areas of the midwest. This
territory in northeastern Ohio was part of the Western Reserve, which
was deeded to Connecticut by Charles II in 1662 and had contained all
land between the forty-first and forty-second parallels from Providence

13. Old photograph of the Kirtland temple, showing simulated bricks

14. Kirtland temple

Plantations to the Pacific Ocean. After independence the grant was abrogated, but Connecticut was given exclusive right to an area of three and a half million acres along the shore line of Lake Erie, where many Connecticut residents settled in the early decades of the nineteenth century. The Kirtland temple shares with the architecture of neighboring Ohio towns a dependence upon architectural forms of Connecticut and western Massachusetts transmitted by way of western New York, where the style, or conglomerate of styles, called Late Colonial, was firmly rooted. Since most of Kirtland was made up of New Yorkers and New Englanders, such borrowings were to be expected, especially by an architecturally inexperienced group.

Clearly, the Mormons did not start out with an *a priori* concept of "style." They simply adopted features of various styles which could be combined to create a beautiful building, following the usual pattern of the migrant, who "tends to construct in his new environment the architectural forms with which he is familiar and that remind him of home . . . not necessarily of the stylistic form current in the parent community."[15] Even the publications of the Saints give surprisingly little information about the building of the temple. The dedication ceremonies of 1836 are reported in great detail, but the architecture itself is mentioned only once in the Mormon periodical *Latter-Day Saints' Messenger and Advocate*, published in Kirtland, and this is only a report of progress in construction and the briefest of descriptions. "It will be lighted with thirty-two Gothic, three Venetian, ten dormer, one circular and two square gable-windows. The dome of the steeple will not be far from 110 feet high, and the bell about 90."[16]

The high rectangular shape, double row of windows, and tower rising from the main body of the building indicate that the general prototype for the temple was the New England meetinghouse. It appears in particular to be a modified version of the typical rural meetinghouse of the post-Revolutionary era, which was customarily arranged with a large assembly hall behind an entrance vestibule extending across the entire width of the building (figure 15). The gallery stairs found at either end of the vestibule in this type were retained in the Kirtland temple, but were used as a means of access to the second floor meeting hall, a feature which replaced the gallery. The belfry is a reduction of the often-seen arrangement of tower over projecting pedimented portico, a type popularized by Bulfinch in his Congregational Church at Pittsfield, Massachusetts, 1790–1793. As described by Kirker, "Bulfinch advanced the once free-standing tower into the body of the building by adding a pedimented porch on the gable end. The main entrance was located in the center of the porch with lesser ones on either side; above the central door he prescribed a Palladian window."[17] The portico has been omitted from the Kirtland temple, but the retention of the three-light window in the center of the facade, in the same position it usually occupied in the entrance portico, suggests

15. Frank Roos, "Ohio: Architectural Cross-road," *Journal of the Society of Architectural Historians* 12, 2 (1953): 3.

16. *Latter-day Saints' Messenger and Advocate* 1, 10 (1835): 147.

17. Harold Kirker, *The Architecture of Charles Bulfinch* (Cambridge, 1969), p. 25.

LONGITUDINAL   SECTION   1-1   TRANSVERSE   SECTION   1-2

VEREDON W UPHAM DEL.

LOOKING WEST | LOOKING EAST

SCALE IN FEET
SCALE IN METRES

*15. Longitudinal and cross-sections of the Kirtland temple, Historic
American Buildings Survey*

the relationship of the temple to the Bulfinch type. This "Venetian" window is obviously derived from the Palladian window, though the higher middle arch has been incorporated into a single pediment which draws all three parts into a unit. Georgian and later colonial churches customarily placed a window behind the pulpit; to accommodate the two-storied arrangement a modified Palladian window is placed behind the pulpit on each floor at the rear of the temple.

The temple's strange appearance is due in part to the lack of any plastic definition of either facades or sides of the building. The smooth, flat surfaces and the regular placement of windows along the flanks lend it a box-like look which is accentuated by the exaggerated quoins at the corners with their naive insistence upon a uniform size for each stone. The quoins, Georgian in origin, seem to act as great hinges connecting the flat planes of the walls. No articulation of the surface by classical orders is seen anywhere on the exterior, probably because of the added cost burden which such decoration would have placed on the already financially hard-pressed community. The Georgian prototypes of the wooden tower are distant and almost unrecognizable, for this tower does not possess any of the baroque plasticity or massiveness of the true Georgian style. The rather delicate and linear carved decoration of the slender tower, the Georgian modillioned pediment and oval pediment window are all quite typical of architecture in the Western Reserve. The facade's lack of unity is symptomatic of the breakdown of the old English classical system, a breakdown illustrated even more strikingly in the intermingling of the Gothic windows with eighteenth-century elements.

The combining of federal and Georgian with Gothic windows was not unique, though it was somewhat unusual. Bulfinch had "Gothicized" his Federal Street Church in Boston by adding pointed windows and transforming the tower into a medieval form by applying finials, tracery, and a pointed spire, while Strickland in Philadelphia was experimenting with Gothic in St. Stephen's Church of 1822–1823. Ithiel Town had introduced Gothic to New Haven at Trinity Church in 1814–1815, another example of Gothic decoration used without a corresponding interest in medieval structural principles. Even the provinces were beginning to respond to changes in architectural fashion. Backwoods Connecticut, for example, saw several churches built which were late colonial in all respects save the pointed windows, and others of this type began to appear in the Western Reserve at about the same time or slightly later than the Kirtland temple.

Besides these very general sources (which there is no evidence that the Mormons may have known), the Kirtland temple is related to another group of churches even closer in appearance, which Smith himself may have seen. On the lower east side of Manhattan there are at least five extant "Georgian Gothic" churches built before 1830. These retain the Georgian proportions and stone construction of

18. Fawn M. Brodie,
*No Man Knows My
History: The Life of
Joseph Smith the
Mormon Prophet*
(London, 1963), p.
123.

eighteenth-century New York churches like St. Paul's Chapel and St. Mark's in the Bouwerie, but they have Gothic windows—as at Kirtland, Gothic in shape only, for they contain colonial mullions rather than medieval tracery. These buildings are abstracted versions of Georgian which in their purity and lack of detail seem to have been affected by the Greek Revival. Most similar to Kirtland are the Northeast Reform Dutch, or Market Street Church (now the Sea and Land Church), built by Henry Rutgers between 1814 and 1817 (figure 16), and All Saints Free Church, 1827–1829. The similarity would have been even greater if the imitation masonry at Kirtland had been preserved. That the Mormons were acquainted with some architecture other than that found in the immediate vicinity of Kirtland, and, in particular, buildings like the two built of random stone, is suggested by the fact that the Kirtland temple was atypical in its use of stone rather than wood, the conventional medium of the Western Reserve.

In October 1832, only half a year before the Kirtland temple began to rise, Joseph Smith visited New York City to secure some loans for the United Order. A letter written to his wife shows how greatly impressed he was by his first contact with a large city:

> This day I have been walking through the most splendid part of the city of New York. The buildings are truly great and wonderful to the astonishing of every beholder. . . . Can the great God of all the earth maker of all things magnificent and splendid be displeased with man for all these great inventions sought out by them. My answer is no it can not be, seeing these great works are calculated to make man comfortable wise and happy, therefore not for these works can the Lord be displeased. Only against man is the anger of the Lord kindled because they give him not glory. . . . Therefore their iniquities shall be visited upon their heads and their works shall be burned up with unquenchable fire.[18]

In this wonderfully ambivalent passage Smith mentions no specific buildings, but he was obviously interested in the architecture. The letter also implies a justification for erecting a building of the size and pretensions of the temple in a poor frontier community. The Lord did not disapprove of magnificent buildings, only the iniquitous men who constructed them. A building consecrated to the Lord, indeed, commanded by the Lord, would serve to increase his glory (and concurrently, Smith's own importance). It is not unlikely that Smith's New York journey inspired him to begin to build up his own town and excited in him a desire to plan a temple comparable to the monuments he had seen in the east, rivalling them as best he could in size and permanence. It should be suitable to serve as the headquarters of the kingdom of the Lord which would in time replace those kingdoms of the world. The above-mentioned Georgian Gothic churches were located in an area which was then fashionable and aristocratic. If Smith

16. Sea and Land Church, New York City

saw them, he may have consciously recollected these buildings when
he included "modern" Gothic windows in the plans for the temple.

To Smith must be attributed the special adaptations which fit the
traditional meetinghouse to specific Mormon requirements. It was in
the interior that features of more originality, which were to become
distinctively Mormon, were introduced. Instead of a single space with
gallery, the temple is divided into two almost identical stories of equal
height. The first floor was intended for worship but the second had a
separate purpose. Proselytizing has always been a major interest of the
Saints, and it was especially important at this time, when converts
were constantly needed simply to insure the progress of the gathering.
The second floor served as a classroom in which men were instructed
before being sent out on missions of conversion. Smith had organized
a "school of the Prophets" for his elders, whose purpose was the study
of the sacred Mormon texts, and this was later expanded to include
classes in Hebrew and Greek as Smith became more involved with the
study of Biblical civilizations. The seats in the second floor hall were
equipped with writing desks for the classes held there during the
week.

The attic is partitioned into ten small rooms, five on either side of a
corridor; these were used as meeting rooms and offices for Smith and
other important church functionaries. It was from his office that Smith
conducted the religious and secular life of the community, and this is
where he worked on his translations and received revelations. The
Kirtland temple was to serve several purposes, then—it was a church,
it was a school, and it was an administrative center. The *Messenger
and Advocate* reported in 1837 that the building was being used in
some capacity every day of the week. In this way it did reflect the
notion of the temple as a multiple-function structure which Smith had
vaguely expressed in his description of the plat of Zion.

The most unusual feature of both meeting halls is the presence
of two complete sets of pulpits in each, one on either end. This arrangement creates a directional tug-of-war which contrasts with the
strongly axial movement of the customary longitudinal church, but
both sets of pulpits were functional and necessary, given the nature of
the Mormon priesthood. Both of the restored priesthoods, the Melchizedek and the Aaronic, had conferred upon them the authority to
conduct meetings and worship services, though never simultaneously.
When the Melchizedek was in charge of the proceedings, the western
pulpits (located where the single pulpit in a church was usually found)
were used, and when the Aaronic priesthood presided, the pews could
be reversed to allow the congregation to face the eastern end, behind
whose pulpits another Venetian window was placed. The window allowed some light to enter from the vestibule and provided a suitably
impressive background. Each pulpit group had a compartment with a
lectern, behind which rose three tiers of pulpits corresponding to the

levels of office within each priesthood (figure 17). This double-ended arrangement was to have ramifications in the Utah temples, where the halls were expressed symbolically on the exterior.

Great care was lavished upon the carved wooden detail of the interior. Eight slender fluted piers support a low ceiling, flat over the aisles and arched over the center. Attenuated and elegant, these are characteristic of post-Revolutionary Adamesque decoration in their noncanonical proportions and highly original classically derived details. Their delicacy is typical of New England late colonial ornament, where "wooden detail became more and more complex and was made of more and more smaller parts; moldings were often tiny, so that the whole effect became sometimes wiredrawn and thin. Columns and pilasters were much slimmer and entablatures proportionately smaller."[19] Here the columns are made even higher by the addition of an impost block above the capital.

The window frames, pulpit ornament (figure 18), and vestibule trimming bespeak the arrival in the Western Reserve of the Greek Revival style, with its fondness for frets and guilloches. Heavier and larger in scale than that of the piers, this type of ornament could have been found in the handbooks of Asher Benjamin, whose works, in editions supplemented by the inclusion of plates with "Greek" details, were being used in Ohio by this time. The 1830 edition of *The Practical House Carpenter* illustrated this kind of detail and contained a design for a pulpit similar to those in the Kirtland temple, though the Kirtland pulpits are more heavily embellished. In general the building is more richly appointed than others of its type; this attention to the interior perhaps results from the greater number of skilled woodworkers than builders in the Mormon community and from the constant use to which the halls would be put as places of business and worship. The second floor decoration is much the same as the first, though it is less elaborate, in keeping with the nature of its use. Both halls are painted white, and though the spaciousness of each is diminished by the low ceilings, the color and the light admitted by the numerous windows complement the tasteful decoration.

A further peculiarity of the interior is the complicated set of ropes and pulleys concealed within the wooden piers, which operated curtains called "veils" that could be lowered to divide each hall into smaller compartments.

> Each [row of pulpits] had curtains hanging from the ceiling overhead down to the top of the pulpit, which could be rolled up or dropped down at pleasure, and when dropped down would completely exclude those within the apartment from the sight of all others. The room was also divided into four compartments by means of curtains or veils hanging from the ceiling overhead down to the floor, so that the house could be used for different purposes.[20]

19. Talbot Hamlin, *Greek Revival Architecture in America* (London, 1944), p. 10.

20. Eliza R. Snow, *Biography and Family Record of Lorenzo Snow* (Salt Lake City, 1884), p. 12.

17. First floor hall, Kirtland temple

18. Pulpit ornament, first floor hall, Kirtland temple

21. Edwin B. Bron-
ner, "Quaker
Landmarks in Early
Philadelphia," in
*Historic Philadel-
phia*, 43, Part I of
*Transactions of
the American
Philosophical Soci-
ety* (Philadelphia,
1953), pp. 120–216.
22. Harold W. Rose,
*The Colonial
Houses of Worship
in America* (New
York, 1963), p. 71.

Veils had been used in the Temple of Solomon and the tabernacle to
isolate the holy area—reserved for members of the priesthood—where
the ark of the covenant was kept, a detail which Smith would certainly
have known. But circumstantial evidence provides a further source for
the veils and pulpits in the Quaker meetinghouse. Quaker communities had developed in the Burned-over District and by the 1830s a
number of Quaker settlements had been established in Ohio. Judging
from the synthesizing abilities Smith displayed in the Book of Mormon, one might also infer that a similar eclectic culling of usable elements was going on in his architectural creation. The following descriptions of a Quaker meetinghouse suggest where Smith may have
derived some of his ideas for the interior of the temple, though this
does not detract from the originality of the combination of items and
especially from the double-ended arrangement:

> Most of the benches faced one direction, but a few benches
> were opposite the others. These were often slightly elevated, and
> were called the gallery or facing benches. Men and women whose
> gift in the ministry had been recognized by their fellow religionists
> sat upon the facing benches. . . .[21]

> Two entrances were provided in one wall, which enabled men
> and women to enter their separate meetings for business simul-
> taneously. A moveable partition down the middle of the audito-
> rium separated the two meetings, and it could be removed for
> meetings of worship.[22]

The second passage quoted above raises an interesting, if ultimately
insoluble question concerning the existence of the two entrance ways.
The Mormons' insistence upon using two doors in all of the Utah temples suggests that they may exist for another reason than to allow access to the double-aisled hall. Multiple doors were often placed on
church facades, but the standard arrangement was three rather than
two doors. The Kirtland temple may have been an adaptation of this
practice, with the elimination of one of the doors occurring much as
other traditional elements had been reduced or eliminated. However, a
two-door disposition was most commonly associated with sects practicing sexual segregation, notably the Shakers and the Quakers. It is
known that in the rooms of the temples in Utah men and women were
segregated, the men always sitting on the right-hand side. As men and
women were also separated during the temple ritual at Nauvoo, it is
tempting to infer that some degree of separation of the sexes also existed at Kirtland. There is no mention in contemporary sources of such
a practice having been instituted this early, although only men were
allowed to attend some of the most important dedication ceremonies
in the Kirtland temple, and there were no offices set up for women in
the Mormon hierarchy. If men and women were indeed isolated at

Kirtland, this would help to explain the seemingly arbitrary placement of the doors and the consequent sacrificing of a balanced disposition of the windows on the facade.

When the building was completed in March 1836, it was dedicated in a frenzy of fervent and emotional worship lasting two weeks. These proceedings reveal something of the attitude the Saints had toward their temple. It was important not so much for its form and style as for the events which occurred within it. The temple seemed to be possessed of its own spirit, to have a sacredness and intrinsic meaning as a holy place. Reports abounded that on the day of dedication and for days preceding it visions had been experienced individually or collectively in the temple, visions in which angels entered, sat among the congregation, and filled the place with supernatural light and sound. People from the neighborhood reported seeing a pillar of fire resting upon the building and those inside were moved to utter prophecies and speak in tongues.

In the dramatic climax of the dedicatory prayers and speeches, Smith and Oliver Cowdery retired behind the veil of the pulpit to pray silently. When the veil was rolled up to the ceiling again, it was apparent to the congregation that both men had been overwhelmed by some great spiritual experience.

> We saw the Lord standing upon the breast-work of the pulpit [Smith wrote in his journal], and under his feet was a paved work of pure gold in color like amber. His eyes were as a flame of fire, the hair of his head was white like the pure snow.

Then the Lord spoke:

> . . . behold, I have accepted this house, and my name shall be here, and I will manifest myself to my people in mercy in this house. . . .

The wonders continued, for

> After this vision closed, the heavens were again opened unto us, and Moses appeared before us, and committed unto us the keys of the gathering of Israel from the four parts of the earth, and the leading of the ten tribes from the land of the north.

Finally, Elijah appeared with a proclamation that the last days were at hand:

> Therefore the keys of this dispensation are committed into your hands, and by this ye may know that the great and dreadful day of the Lord is near, even at the doors.[23]

The apparition of Elijah in the temple was a brilliant gesture by Smith designed to impress upon his audience the importance of his

23. Joseph Smith, *History of the Church*, II, pp. 432–434; *Doctrine and Covenants* 110.

leadership and of the temple, for it was the fulfillment of the last prophecy of the Old Testament, found in Malachi 4:5–6:

> Behold, I will send you Elijah the prophet, before the coming of the great and dreadful day of the Lord:
> And he shall turn the heart of the fathers to the children, and the heart of the children to their fathers, lest I come and smite the earth with a curse.

Smith's vision implied that a significant state had now been attained. An authentic temple existed, where Christ could manifest himself, its dedication had inaugurated the last days, and the Lord's authority had been officially restored to the first genuine prophet since Biblical times. The specific association of the temple with the Parousia and the gathering and its position as an essential communicative link between God and man made it imperative always to have a temple. Somehow, these great events could not transpire without a properly sanctified edifice set apart from the mundane world.

The fairly traditional appearance of the Kirtland temple is an accurate reflection of the uncomplicated Mormon theological tenets of the 1830s. For all practical purposes the temple was a meetinghouse, with some changes made to adapt the form to innovations in the organization of the church, that was rather more crudely finished on the exterior than churches of more well-established denominations. As far as the nature of worship was concerned, there was little ritual when the building was begun. The introduction of a footwashing ceremony took place in 1833, but others were inaugurated only after the temple had been completed. The ceremonies have been interpreted by Brodie as resulting from Smith's need to institute special rituals worthy of the building. He had promised his followers that great blessings would be theirs when the temple was completed as a palliative to those who objected to committing resources to such an extravagant project. The conferring of endowments, anointing with oil, and the "sealing" ceremony, by which the blessings called down upon the heads of those present in the endowment ritual were sealed in heaven for eternity, were thus grafted onto Latter-day Saint practice and did not affect in any way the planning of the temple.

The Saints were able to enjoy their new temple for only a short time. Early in 1838 most of the inhabitants of Kirtland left Ohio for the Missouri settlement, a flight precipitated by the disastrous failure in January 1837 of the Kirtland Safety Society Anti-Banking Company, which had been issuing bank notes without coin reserves supporting them. When the nationwide panic hit in the spring, the church was threatened with disintegration. It was already heavily in debt—due in no small amount to the construction of the temple, which was mortgaged for about $20,000—and its land values were falling rapidly. Missouri, where questions of land ownership and value were more casual, held out the hope of saving the church financially and preserving unity and loyalty to Smith, for the Mormons were racked with schism and apostasy. Missouri was to be no sanctuary, though, for the Missourians were suspicious of and hostile towards the nonslaveholding Mormons. The gentiles were alarmed by the Mormons' acting as a body to purchase large areas of land, and by their excessive friendliness towards the "Lamanites." In 1833 the Mormons had been driven from Independence north to Clay County, then in 1836 to Caldwell County, where they were joined by Smith's group. Here one last gesture was made towards erecting a temple in Eden.

In the summer of 1837 it was resolved that a house of the Lord should be constructed at Far West, with a revelation in April 1838 stating that a pattern would be given by the Lord (and this time the Lord specified that no debts were to be incurred on his account). The site was dedicated and the cornerstone laid on 4 July 1838, and this was the last work done. Since it was obvious to the Saints that their days in Missouri were numbered, no preparations for construction were made. In October 1838 Governor Lilburn Boggs issued the infamous "order of extermination," which directed the raising of four hundred armed men to forcibly expel, and, if necessary, exterminate the Mormons. Conceding, the Mormons moved across the Mississippi to Illinois, leaving the Far West temple, as they had left the one at Independence, to be built by a future generation.

Chapter 4

Ritual and Symbolism at Nauvoo

Nauvoo, Illinois, was host in 1844 to two aristocratic gentlemen from the east who were on a tour of the country. Josiah Quincy and Charles Francis Adams received courteous attention and a personal tour of the city from its mayor, Joseph Smith. As Quincy reported in his journal:

> The clouds had parted when we emerged from the chamber of curiosities[1] and there was time to see the Temple before dinner. General Smith ordered a capacious carriage, and we drove to that beautiful eminence, bounded on three sides by the Mississippi, which was covered by the holy city of Nauvoo. The curve in the river enclosed a position lovely enough to furnish a site for the utopian communities of Plato and Sir Thomas More; and here was an orderly city, magnificently laid out, and teeming with enterprise. And all the diligent workers, who had reared these handsome stores and comfortable dwellings, bowed in subjection to the man to whose unexampled absurdities we had listened that morning.[2]

The impression which Nauvoo made upon Quincy was a tribute to the tenacity of Smith's vision of the gathering. Far from abandoning his dream of a community of the elect, even after having seen three such settlements dispersed through a combination of outside harassment and intramural dissension, Smith insisted that his people maintain their identity as a group. If, upon leaving Missouri, the Mormons had scattered to various parts of the midwest, pressure from fearful gentiles would doubtless have lessened, for the objectionable characteristics of Mormonism depended significantly upon its acting in concert in such crucial matters as land purchase. By giving up the gathering, the Mormons would have become enough like other religious groups to no longer pose a threat to their neighbors, but this capitulation would certainly have destroyed their cohesiveness as well as the primary reason for the new religion's existence. Instead, Smith regrouped his flock in and around Quincy, Illinois, while he negotiated for land. The local residents welcomed the Mormons, sympathizing with them for their misfortunes, and both political parties eagerly anticipating the

1. The chamber of curiosities was a room in Smith's house containing four mummies and several rolls of papyrus which the church had bought at Kirtland. Visitors paid a quarter to see them.

2. Josiah Quincy, *Figures of the Past* (Boston, 1883), in William Mulder and A. Russell Mortensen, eds., *Among the Mormons* (New York, 1958), p. 137.

effect of such a large body of new voters on state elections. By early 1839 a small group of houses on the eastern side of the Mississippi just north of the Iowa-Missouri boundary—whose name had previously been changed from Venus to Commerce—had been renamed, this time Nauvoo, meaning "a beautiful plantation" in revised Hebrew, or so Smith told the Saints who began to move there with what meager possessions they had managed to bring from Missouri.

No one, with the exception of Smith himself, could have foreseen in the site the potential for the city which Adams and Quincy visited, for as it existed in 1839, Nauvoo was a peninsula of malarial marsh separated from the higher prairie on the east by a meandering line of low bluffs. Yet by the following year the Prophet's expectations began to be fulfilled, as the marshes were drained, the city platted, and houses put up. By the time of the assassination of Smith and his brother Hyrum in 1844, Nauvoo boasted a population of over eleven thousand within the city itself and a third of that number outside its limits; it included land across the river in Iowa where subsidiary communities were being established. If these figures, claimed by the Mormon press in Nauvoo, are correct, the city would at that time have surpassed Chicago in population.

Spectacular as Nauvoo's growth was, to some extent it was deceptive, for sheer numbers did not necessarily insure a vigorous economic life. As soon as Smith had decided that Nauvoo was to be the new headquarters of the church, word went out that the gathering was to be effected immediately. Communications to the eastern Saints stressed the urgency of selling land and possessions and moving to Nauvoo, instructions which a great many obeyed. But even more important was the phenomenal success of the British Mission. During the troubles in Kirtland, Smith had set up the British Mission as a way to maintain the loyalty of some of his most important elders by sending them away while he tried to extricate himself from the financial and legal morass in which the church found itself. Attracted not only by the promise of salvation but by glowing reports of the abundant and productive land which each man could own (the *Millennial Star*, published in Liverpool, reported in February 1842 that around Nauvoo there were "thousands and millions of acres of beautiful prairie, unoccupied, which can be procured on reasonable terms"), British converts, many of them indigents from the urban slums, organized themselves into groups and chartered ships to America. Landing at New Orleans and then securing river transport to Nauvoo, the immigrants came at a rate which increased annually to the peak year of 1843, which saw twelve hundred new inhabitants arrive at the Mormon city. Nauvoo, whose sole basis for existence was religious, was an artificial creation with no foundation in commerce or manufacturing; moreover an unusual number of its members could not contribute capital or skills. Its return to somnolence after the Mormon exodus is indicative of the limited possibilities which this location offered.

As it appeared on Gustavus Hills's map of 1842 (figure 19), the city resembled Independence in its relentless grid pattern of residential blocks. But the center was no longer to be reserved for temples and public buildings, as had been intended at Zion. The map gives no indication that any public buildings were projected; indeed there was apparently no center of town and no main streets. The one building which was planned from the beginning was the temple, but rather than forming the nucleus of an agrarian community, its site was to be on top of the bluff overlooking the town, on land which was not even owned by the church at that time. The temple was without doubt the most important part of the city, and its prominent location above the flatlands where houses were being built was a manifestation of the greater role which architecture was to play at Nauvoo. Dominating the landscape, the temple would convey to all a sense that this was the holy city.

The revelation about the Nauvoo temple came in January 1841, but Joseph Smith had already begun talking about the necessity of building it the previous year, first referring to it in August and then again in October, in an epistle to the Twelve Apostles who were carrying out missionary work in Britain:

> You will observe . . . that we are about building a temple for the worship of God in this place. Preparations are now making; every tenth day is devoted by the brethren for quarrying rock, in this region of the country. It is expected to be considerably larger than the one in Kirtland, and on a more magnificent scale, and which will undoubtedly attract the attention of the great men of the earth.[3]

It is clear that besides serving as a place of worship, the temple was meant to entice people to the Mormon camp and to firmly establish Mormonism as a religion of some permanence and pretensions. In the same month the revelation was issued a letter appeared in the Saints' newspaper, *Times and Seasons*, from a non-Mormon who had dealings with the Saints, reinforcing Smith's views. The writer urged the construction of a temple "that for size, proportions and style shall attract, surprise and dazzle all beholders . . . unique externally, and on the interior peculiar, imposing and grand."[4] In fact, so concerned was Smith with the impression that his city and temple would have upon visitors that in the same revelation the Lord also directed the construction of a hotel, Nauvoo House. It was to lodge those who would come to marvel at Zion, as Smith now began to call Nauvoo, and hopefully to function as a successful commercial venture as well.

The unusual relationship of the temple to the uniquely combined

3. Smith, *History of the Church*, IV, p. 229.
4. *Times and Seasons*, 9 January, 1841.

19. Gustavus Hills's map of Nauvoo

religious-secular aspect of life in Nauvoo is clearly indicated by noting that the Saints, during their entire eight years in Nauvoo, never built a church or chapel for worship services, even though the number of people in the area might have seemed to require it. All efforts were directed—as far as religious building was concerned—towards the temple. Congregations of the people on Sundays and special occasions were held in the open air until the summer of 1845, when a canvas "tabernacle" was set up in front of the partially completed temple wherein to hold meetings. Within a year after the Mormons settled Nauvoo, the holy city was beginning to take on the character of a quasi-independent city-state, a situation which helps to explain the dramatic location and large size of the temple (approximately one hundred twenty-eight by eighty-eight feet) and also its undisputed primacy as the major architectural endeavor of the new Zion. Much less attention was given to domestic buildings, which were small and quite primitive, as can be seen in a photograph taken sometime between 1846 and 1848 (figure 20).

Having learned from the experience in Missouri that the legal apparatus of the United States government could not be relied upon to champion the rights of his minority, Smith had determined to provide Nauvoo with an adequate measure of self-protection. Taking advantage of the eagerness of the Illinois politicians to woo the Mormon vote, which was sizeable enough to exert considerable influence upon state elections, the Mormons were able to manoeuvre through the state legislature a city charter conferring extraordinary powers upon the Mormon hierarchy, who naturally held the important city offices in Nauvoo. Passed in December 1840 by a majority of both parties, the charter gave the nod to a collusion between judicial and municipal branches of government. Providing for the mayor of the city to act also as the chief justice of the municipal court, while aldermen were justices of the peace and associates justices of the court, the charter in effect gave the Latter-day Saints the power to make their own laws and enforce them. More important, the city's court was empowered to issue writs of *habeas corpus*, which could be used to free arrested persons anywhere in the state of Illinois, thus assuring Mormons sanctuary in their own city. By virtue of this measure Joseph Smith was no longer subject to gentile arrest and imprisonment, something which had happened more than once while the Saints were in Missouri.

In their eagerness to curry favor with the Mormons, the Illinois legislators also granted Nauvoo permission to organize its own militia, under the command not of the state militia, as was customary, but of the mayor of the city, who was to use it to enforce the laws of the city so long as they were not antipathetical to the state constitution. The Nauvoo Legion by the beginning of 1842 had two thousand armed and well-drilled men under the leadership of self-appointed Lieutenant-General Joseph Smith, the only person in the United States to hold this

20. *Nauvoo, Illinois*

rank. Since Smith gave orders which could only be countermanded by the governor of the state, Nauvoo was effectively protected from interference by the gentile world.[5] The Mormons quickly came to regard the Nauvoo Legion not as a civil militia but as their own religious battalion, whose primary obligation was the protection of Nauvoo and its inhabitants rather than loyalty to the state government. The temple on the bluff as a manifestation of the authority of the church was not, then, without a basis in actuality. The Latter-day Saints had indeed, within a rather circumscribed area, made the great men of the earth take notice.

The construction of the temple was carried out under the supervision of a special temple committee, and for this building Smith did employ an architect to draw up plans for him and oversee the building site. The temple committee had evidently begun the construction of the temple, which was to be similar to Kirtland, but the basement was "much botched" by them.[6] Smith does not mention the name of his architect until 1843, but from context it is clear that this person had been the temple architect for some time and was given total control over the building as a result of the spoiling of the foundations:

> In consequence of misunderstanding on the part of the Temple committee, and their interference with the business of the architect, I gave a certificate to William Weeks to carry out my designs on the architecture of the Temple in Nauvoo, and that no person or persons shall interfere with him or his plans in the building of the Temple.[7]

The scanty information about William Weeks's life offers no clue as to what architectural training (if any) he may have had or what buildings he saw or worked on before coming to Nauvoo. All that is known is that he was born on Martha's Vineyard on 11 April 1813, and then is lost sight of until June 1839, when his marriage ceremony was performed by a Mormon elder in Quincy, Illinois. His presence in Illinois at so early a date suggests that he may have been with the Saints in Missouri. His name is not mentioned before this, and he is not on the list of those who worked on the Kirtland temple, so he might have been a fairly recent convert. Weeks left Nauvoo with the rest of the Mormon population in 1846 at the request of Brigham Young, who wanted him to design a temple at whatever location the Saints made their new home. He was in Utah in 1847, and for the next decade he led a peripatetic life, returning to the east in June 1848, back to Provo, Utah, in 1853, and then moving to San Bernardino, California, where there was a colony of Mormons. Though this colony was subsequently abandoned, Weeks remained in California, moving to the Los Angeles area, where he designed flour and saw mills. He died in 1900. In his later life his connection with Mormonism was peripheral at best. He had nothing to do with the planning of any of the Utah temples, and the

5. The Nauvoo Legion was not the first instance of Smith's resorting to military force to protect the interests of the church. An abortive expedition known as Zion's Camp had been organized in 1834, when Smith took about two hundred men by foot from Kirtland to Jackson County to try to preserve the existence of Zion at Independence. When the "army" arrived, Smith quickly realized the futility of the endeavor of his badly outnumbered group and dissolved Zion's Camp before any battles took place. However, the precedent for an army of the Lord had been set.

6. Letter from Truman O. Angell to John Taylor, 11 March, 1885, in the Church Historian's Office in Salt Lake City.

7. Smith, *History of the Church*, V, p. 353.

8. Smith, *History of the Church*, VI, p. 196.

Nauvoo temple is the only building of any importance with which his name can be positively connected.

From the evidence of the temple itself, it would seem more accurate to call Weeks a builder rather than an architect; an architect with any kind of professional training in this part of the country at such an early date, associated with a fringe sect, would have been unusual in the extreme. The carpenter-builder was the most common architect of this time and place. The construction of the temple was unlike most frontier building programs, however, for there are a number of preliminary drawings which have been preserved in good condition. The evolution of the Nauvoo temple as seen in these drawings offers a unique opportunity to study the coming of age of a frontier builder-architect as he worked towards a satisfactory accommodation of architectural tradition with a desire for original expression. Weeks's designs demonstrate his familiarity with the traditions of New England, but they also record the influx of modern ideas of the 1840s as transmitted primarily through the medium of architectural handbooks. His final plans do not depend on a specific source and are novel in their adaptation of architectural motifs. They demonstrate, by comparison with the earlier plans, a greater proficiency in handling the architectural vocabulary.

But what of Smith's role in the planning of the building, and how did he maintain any pretense of the Lord's having inspired the structure while at the same time employing a professional architect? He continued to tout his powers as a prophet by proclaiming that the plans had been given to him in a revelation, which his architect then put into effect. Since there already were certain prerequisites for a Mormon temple which had been instituted at Kirtland (two stories, a double-ended meeting hall) and which Smith imposed upon his architect's designs, the belief fostered by the Prophet that Weeks drafted the plans under his dictation is no doubt true to a certain extent, but the building from its earliest stages clearly manifests a more sophisticated acquaintance with architectural styles than Smith and his associates had exhibited at Kirtland. One is tempted to be wary of the story in Smith's *History* of the confrontation between himself and Weeks over the inclusion of round windows in the mezzanine story of the temple elevation. As Smith would have it, Weeks was prevailed upon to make the windows round instead of semicircular, even though Weeks thought this feature to be a "violation of all the known rules of architecture."[8] However this altercation took place in 1844, some two years after Weeks's first drawings—with round windows—had been submitted. Perhaps Smith was altering the facts slightly to suit his conception of himself as supreme architectural dictator, especially since he intended his journals to become part of the public literature of the church. The most plausible assessment of each man's part in the building is to assign to Weeks those elements which are purely architectural, while crediting the determination of functional and symbolic requirements to the president himself.

Three drawings of the Nauvoo temple are in the Church Historian's Office in Salt Lake City. One of these is not actually a drawing from which the architect worked—it is the inset perspective rendering of the temple, bearing William Weeks's signature, which appeared on Gustavus Hills's map of the city (figure 21). This is thought to have been printed in mid-1842 and was sold in Nauvoo for fifty cents. The second (figure 22), an architect's drawing, is neither signed nor dated, but the draftsmanship is the same as that of an undated, but signed, drawing by Weeks (figure 23). The signed drawing is the last in the series, so placed because of the substitution of the oblong attic story for the triangular pediment. This is the form of the temple as it was built; though some changes were made between the last drawing and the actual building, these are confined largely to the tower and do not substantially affect the overall design. A daguerreotype of the finished building (figure 24) records how it looked sometime before 1848, when the building was gutted by fire. After the Mormons departed from Nauvoo, the temple was taken over by a group of French communists, who began to rebuild it to use as a school. When a tornado struck it in 1850, what remained of the walls was torn down and used as building material in and around Nauvoo; some of the limestone blocks can still be seen in the walls of houses and stores in the town. The foundation of the temple was recently excavated (figure 25) and there are several capitals and bases of the pilasters still in Illinois (figures 26 and 27).

The engraving on Hills's map presents a building which, despite its pilasters, bears witness to the longevity of the eighteenth-century meetinghouse. The body of the temple is related to Kirtland in its double-storied arrangement, but has taken on Greek Revival proportions, with two additional bays and a broader facade than the first temple. In a strikingly awkward intermingling of forms, Weeks set an immense tower over the facade immediately behind the pediment. This in itself was not startling, since this was the usual place for a tower in a Georgian church, but in combination with a Greek temple base instead of a Georgian portico, the heavy tower contradicts the inherent horizontality and balance of the classical mode. Weeks also simply ignored the problem of relating the facade to the sides at the corners, a problem caused by the use of pilasters instead of free-standing columns. The pilasters practically collide at the corners, but do not quite meet, leaving the corner of the building protruding beyond them, whereas in a building with a colonnade the corner columns would simultaneously act as the end columns of both facade and side.

No specific source can be found for the details of the first design of the temple, but this is to be expected, given the nature of the building

THE TEMPLE. NAUVOO;   Drawn by W Weeks Nauvoo

21. Drawing of the temple, from Hills's map of Nauvoo

22. *Preliminary design for the Nauvoo temple*

23. Preliminary design for the Nauvoo temple

24. Daguerreotype of the Nauvoo temple

25. *Foundations of the Nauvoo temple*

26. *Capital from the Nauvoo temple*

27. *Pilaster base from the Nauvoo temple*

practice in the 1840s. As has been pointed out many times, Greek Revival builders, especially in provincial areas, did not insist upon a canonical use of the orders and eschewed exact replicas of antique buildings, preferring a more imaginative approach in which the vocabulary of classicism could be adapted to a variety of uses. Weeks turned, for his first attempt at monumental building, not to an ancient structure, but to that ubiquitous source of eighteenth- and early nineteenth-century church architecture, James Gibbs's St. Martin's-in-the-Fields, to which he applied a veneer of "Greek" details and otherwise modified. Several elements of the engraving suggest that he was attempting a free interpretation of St. Martin's as it appeared in Gibbs's *A Book of Architecture* of 1728. Plate I (figure 28) in Gibbs's book is a perspective view seen from exactly the same vantage-point as the Nauvoo temple on the map. Both are set on a low base with a broad stairway approaching the entrance, and both have a hexastyle facade and two stories of round-arched windows on the side elevation. A most convincing similarity is a rather minor feature, the balustrade along the side roof of the Nauvoo temple which abruptly runs into the pediment just after turning the corner at the facade. This is not a Greek Revival detail, nor was it usually found on Georgian churches in America. It does occupy precisely the same position as its counterpart in the Gibbs engraving.[9]

The four-story tower is also descended from the London building, though again the relationship is distant. The tower of St. Martin's rises in a tier of three rectangular blocks to the circular base of the spire, a proportional arrangement which Weeks also adopts in his drawing. A low base on the Nauvoo tower with three circular decorative devices, evidently an elaboration of the single roundel on the tower base of St. Martin's, supports a second story, approximately cubic, which is surmounted by a clock story. In place of the spire, the American architect has substituted a square, federal-style cupola, much less "churchy" than the emphatically Christian steeple. The tower exhibits no free-standing columns, only pilasters, and there are, in fact, no freestanding columns anywhere on the building. With its resultant desiccated classicism, this first proposal for the Nauvoo temple is closer in feeling to pre-Greek Revival architecture than is at first apparent. The tower seems to suggest even earlier sources than the Gibbsian churches in America, particularly the nonecclesiastical colonial structures like Independence Hall in Philadephia.

Even in the fuzzy print on Hills's map it is apparent that the pilasters do not really conform to any of the classical orders. Their bases are crescent moons, and the capitals, though they are not yet the sun faces which appear on the other drawings, certainly possess some kind of applied ornament resembling the two heavenly hands holding trumpets seen on the capitals as they were carved. The progressive changes in the two additional drawings reaffirm the chronological arrangement

9. A similar balustrade on Peter Harrison's King's Chapel is believed to have been adapted from St. Martin's. See Priscilla Metcalf, "Boston Before Bulfinch: Harrison's King's Chapel," *Journal of the Society of Architectural Historians*, 13, 1 (1954): 11–14.

28. St. Martins-in-the-Fields

of the drawings for the temple. As it was built, the temple belonged to an "order" consisting of sunface capitals surmounted by hands holding trumpets, anthropoid inverted crescent moons as bases, and five-pointed stars which served as triglyphs. The drawing closest in appearance to the completed temple, with rectangular attic story (figure 23), possesses this complete order; the Hills drawing has neither sun faces nor stars, and while the remaining drawing does have the faces, it lacks the star triglyphs and so must occupy an intermediate position between the map illustration and the signed drawing.

The basic elements of the Hills engraving are retained in the second temple drawing, with some changes effected in the tower. It is now possible to see the details of the pilasters more clearly, as well as the ashlar surface of the facade of the building's lower portion. The patterned voussoirs of the doors and windows, a reduction and regularization of the heavily rusticated apertures of St. Martin's, make the building richer and more decorative. But it is in the tower that Weeks begins to experiment with his forms and ornament and to try to adjust the tower to the base of the temple. The first stage of the tower is lower, with the circular motifs replaced by rectangular panels, and the Doric order has been applied with greater consistency to the second and fourth stories. The substitution of a rounded cupola for the pointed one of the first drawing and the gradual transition from square base to octagonal clock section to cylindrical cupola is another endeavor to harmonize all parts as well as possible.

Far more interesting changes occur in the third drawing. The facade is identical with that of the second drawing up to the level of the entablature, where Weeks has now become more proper in his interpretation of the classical vocabulary, for the quasi-Ionic entablature of the two earlier drawings is now undoubtedly an original interpretation of Doric, with appropriately uninterrupted architrave and division of the frieze into "triglyphs" and metopes (the round windows). But the triangular pediment has given way to an eccentric and nonclassical rectangular attic story, five bays wide and two deep. A vaguely classical cast is given to this area by the pilasters which separate the fenestrated square bays, but the semicircular windows are also unusual. Weeks's reason for making this change cannot be known for sure, but two possibilities suggest themselves. One is simply that as he gained more confidence and practice, the builder sought a more original design, something which would set this Mormon temple apart from Christian churches and at the same time belong to Weeks's own personal style. On the other hand, this feature may have been demanded by Smith. As will be explained later in this chapter, the attic of the temple was functional and played an important role in Mormon religious ritual towards the end of the stay at Nauvoo. The rectangular attic would have been practical, since it allowed for the inclusion of several more rooms than could have been accommodated under a slanting roof.

29. St. Pancras

The tower exhibits a major alteration, for the entire shape has become an octagon. Freestanding columns are placed at each angle of the major story and slight changes are evident in the cupola decoration. As a result, it is no longer recognizably a derivative of St. Martin's and more closely approaches the Greek Revival style of the 1840s. The drawing itself shows a new interest in plasticity and mass, for the architect has heavily shaded the left side of the tower to indicate the effect of light and shadow. Beneath all this, however, it is still possible to detect a model, again an English building. There is no definitive evidence that William Weeks had access to Britton and Pugin's *Illustrations of the Public Buildings of London*, Volume I published in London in 1825 and the second appearing in 1828, but there is a strong possibility that he did, especially considering the influx of English converts to Nauvoo at the time of the temple's planning and the close communications between Nauvoo and the British Mission. Volume I contains plates and description of the church of St. Pancras (figure 29) designed by the Inwoods in 1818, illustrating this building's very prominent use of the octagonal tower. Another popular book, James Elmes's *Metropolitan Improvements*, published in 1827, also illustrated St. Pancras. The octagonal tower rising in progressively smaller stages to a spire had been used in the seventeenth century by Wren, but St. Pancras is Greek Revival. Modifying the older form to reflect the new interest in antique monuments stimulated by archaeological publications, the Inwoods quoted the Tower of the Winds in Athens, an octagon, for the two major stages of the tower, and added freestanding columns, possibly from another antique source, the Choregic Monument of Lysicrates.

John Summerson and Marcus Whiffen[10] have demonstrated that many London churches of the second decade of the nineteenth century, including St. Pancras, were in actuality not so much the descendants of Wren's buildings as of St. Martin's and addressed themselves to the same, perhaps insoluble, problem of reconciling a classical portico with a Christian tower, but with more concern for archaeological accuracy. The Nauvoo temple, then, in spite of many alterations, adheres to the tradition of St. Martin's and the Gibbsian type, but updates it. Most professional architects had access to the books mentioned, which were used to introduce current English fashions into American building. (Minard Lafever, in one instance, appropriated and modified Robert Smirke's St. Mary's Church, Bryanston Square, Marylebone, from Britton and Pugin, and included it as an example of a "Church in the Ionic Order" in his *Young Builder's General Instructor*.) Taking into consideration the time lag between east coast and the frontier in the absorption of new architectural styles, Weeks would have been quite progressive in his use of a modern English source for the tower of the temple.

The reference to two English buildings, St. Martin's and St. Pan-

10. John Summerson, *Georgian London* (London, 1970), p. 91; Marcus Whiffen, "The Progeny of St. Martins-in-the-Fields," *Architectural Review*, 100, 595 (1946): 3–6.

11. Smith, *History of the Church*, VI, p. 197.

cras, for the basic form of the temple implies something about the nature and aspirations of the Mormons at Nauvoo. Both of these churches were pretentious and extremely costly city churches, conceived on a scale far grander than the plans Smith had envisioned for Independence and Kirtland. However by 1841, the date of the revelation commanding the building of the temple, Joseph Smith was no longer interested in an exclusively agrarian community. The utopia which was being established at Nauvoo was not in the wilderness, but was part of the bustling and populated semifrontier. The Mormon settlement had by this time taken on a distinctly urban character which necessitated a temple of fittingly imposing dimensions and form which could not be obtained by merely applying details from handbooks to a simple box shape such as Kirtland had been.

The daguerreotype in the Missouri Historical Society (figure 24), taken sometime between 1846 and 1848, shows the temple as it looked when the Saints abandoned their city to make the final move to Utah. The building faced west, overlooking the Mississippi, just at the point where the hill upon which it sat sloped down towards the flatlands below. The building material was native gray limestone quarried not far from the city. Polished stone pilasters articulated the flanks into nine bays and the facade into five. The side elevation was very similar to the earliest drawing by Weeks, though the addition of the circular windows in the entablature transformed the building into a four-story structure of two major and two minor divisions. Other changes are the wider proportions of the tower and the pointed arches it contained, the square rather than semicircular attic windows, and the inscription added to the central bay of the attic identifying the building and giving the date of its beginning, as had been done on the Kirtland temple.

The triple-arched entranceway led into a vestibule with circular staircases at either end, though the actual entrance to the first-floor hall was through two doors (figure 30). On the interior the resemblance to Kirtland was striking (figure 31). The hall of each of the two main stories had an arched ceiling and the first floor exhibited the double-ended arrangement of three rows of pulpits to seat the two priesthoods (the second floor remained uncompleted). As at Kirtland, the reversible backs of the seats allowed the congregation to face either east or west. In the reconstruction of the Nauvoo temple by Southern Illinois University's archaeological expedition, the space over the side aisles in each story formed a mezzanine floor divided into small rooms corresponding to the round windows, seven on each side, so that "one light at the center of each circular window would be sufficient to light the whole room; that when the whole building was thus illuminated, the effect would be remarkably grand."[11] The main attic under the sloping roof contained a long central room with twelve side chambers, and the higher western end enclosed a single room divided by fabric curtains into three smaller rooms.

30. Engraving of the Nauvoo temple ruins, from John Hyde,
Mormonism: Its Leaders and Designs, *1857*

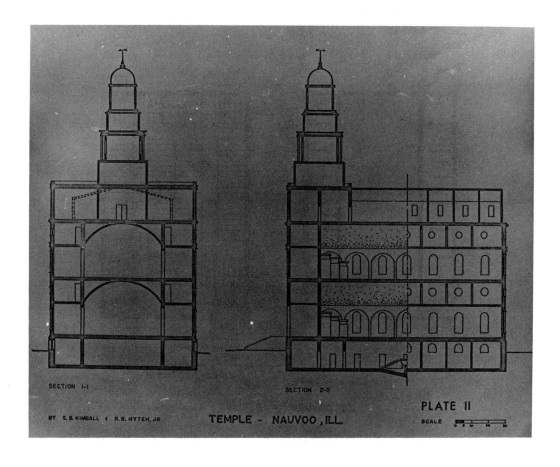

31. Longitudinal and cross-sections of the Nauvoo temple, as reconstructed by Southern Illinois University

With its double-storied, double-ended interior, the Nauvoo temple would seem to have been functionally similar to Kirtland as a place of worship and instruction and as an administrative center for the church hierarchy. But the commandment to erect the temple, the first occasion upon which the Lord had been moved to speak since 1839, included within it sanction of a practice which had been going on for some time in Nauvoo, and specified a new function for the temple:

> For a baptismal font there is not upon the earth, that they, my saints, may be baptized for those who are dead. . . .
>
> For this ordinance belongeth to my house, and cannot be acceptable to me, only in the days of your poverty, wherein ye are not able to build a house unto me. . . .
>
> For verily I say unto you, that after you have had sufficient time to build a house unto me, wherein the ordinances of baptizing for the dead belongeth, and for which the same was instituted from before the foundation of the world, your baptism for your dead cannot be acceptable unto me.[12]

The dramatic increase in the number of his followers and the relative security which this almost totally Mormon town enjoyed had allowed Joseph Smith the freedom to expand upon his religious dogma, assured as he was of a faithful congregation which had accepted his testimony as the word of God. Immersion of living proxy for those who had died before the reestablishment of the legitimate church and who therefore had missed the opportunity for redemption had been taught publicly at Nauvoo since August 1840, about the time that Smith began discussing the future temple there. Baptism in this case was performed not for the absolution of original sin—which Smith had rejected—but for the remission of sins which had been committed during one's earthly life. These rites took place in the Mississippi River until forbidden by Smith in October 1841. Interestingly, and in keeping with the pattern of ritual established at Kirtland, where female participation in the significant religious ceremonies was proscribed, men were baptized for both male and female dead.

The new revelation made it clear that this ordinance was to be transferred to the temple, and further instructions were given in September 1842 for the maintenance of an official recorder to witness and record the baptisms, "That in all your recordings it may be recorded in heaven; that whosoever you bind on earth, may be bound in heaven."[13] These records were to be stored in the archives of the temple, where a baptismal font would be located. Smith claimed that baptism for the dead was a necessary step in bringing about the new dispensation of the last days, that man must be made perfect through association with all of mankind, that ". . . the earth will be smitten with a curse unless there is a welding link of some kind or other between the fathers and the children."[14] He envisioned a vast chain of humankind stretching

12. *Doctrine and Covenants* 124: 29–33.
13. *Ibid.*, 127:7.
14. *Ibid.*, 128:18.

15. *Ibid.*
16. Thomas F. O'Dea, *The Mormons* (Chicago, 1957), p. 57.
17. *Doctrine and Covenants* 128:13.
18. Henry Halkett's Notes Upon Joe Smith the Prophet, 1844, Clements Library, University of Michigan.

from Adam to the present day, uniting all in a "whole and complete and perfect union."[15]

The instituting of baptism for the dead as a means of uniting man with his ancestors has been interpreted as an expression of a need for historical continuity and for the creation of some kind of past tradition to more closely connect Mormonism with its Biblical precursors, the early Christians and Hebrews (Smith had taken the idea of the linkage of fathers and children from Malachi 4:5–6 and regarded the new baptism as the fulfillment of this text). It provided at the same time a greater number who could be counted among the ranks of the Saints. "It seems that at the very time when Mormonism was in fact and belief immensely widening the chasm that separated the converted from the general run of their fellows, there was needed some countermotion, some symbolic link between the separated and their own past in terms of relatives and ancestors."[16] In addition baptism for the dead was, in Smith's eyes, more authentic than baptism practiced by the other churches and provided an opportunity to redo history, to eradicate past evil, and to prepare for the recreation of the American Eden, populated by Adam and his resurrected descendants, all of whom would, through baptism for the dead, be incorporated into the new society.

Before any of the temple superstructure was begun, a basement was completed and dedicated in November 1841. It was designated as the location for the font because, "the baptismal font was instituted as a similitude of the grave, and was commanded to be in a place underneath where the living are wont to assemble, to show forth the living and the dead. . . ."[17] This was used while the rest of the building was being constructed, and it is thus apparent that baptism for the dead had always been considered as part of the ceremonies of the temple, and perhaps the most important rite. A temporary font was housed in a wooden shed in the basement until more permanent shelter could be provided. As described in the *History of the Church*, the font was oval-shaped, made of pine wood, and stood eleven feet high. It rested upon twelve wooden oxen, whose head, shoulders, and front legs projected out from beneath the basin. This was seen by Josiah Quincy when he visited Nauvoo, and he characterized it as a "large fine tub supported on twelve oxen carved in imitation of the Jewish original."[18]

If Quincy made the above remark to Smith, the prophet must have been pleased that his visitor had recognized the prototype, for it was indeed patterned after that appointment of King Solomon's temple described in I Kings; it added another note of authenticity to the structure. Smith even boasted to his visitors that he was greater than Solomon, for he was building his temple at Nauvoo without any help, while the Biblical king had been aided by Hiram of Tyre. The *Times and Seasons* of 15 January 1845 reported that the wooden font was being replaced by one of stone, designed by Weeks. Henry Lewis sketched it in 1848, showing it to have been an oval basin set upon the

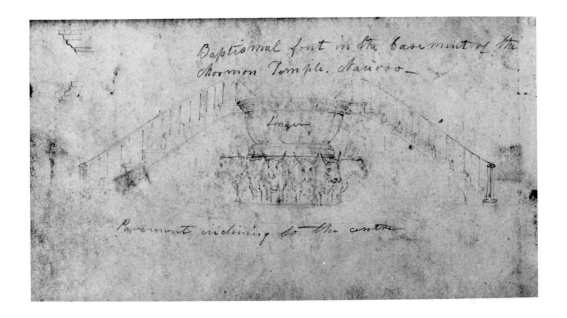

32. *Henry Lewis's drawing of the baptismal font in the Nauvoo temple*

19. Irene Hascall to Ashbel G. Hascall, 2 June, 1845, Southern Illinois University at Edwardsville microfilm collection.
20. Irene Hascall to Ursula B. Hascall, 26 July, 1845, Southern Illinois University at Edwardsville.

backs of oxen, approached by stairways on either side (figure 32). Other visitors reported that the ears and horns of the oxen were made of tin, and the stone of the base was carved in imitation of drapery, from which the oxen seemed to be emerging. After the Mormons left Nauvoo, the font was desecrated by the neighboring populace and further destroyed by the fire of 1848.

After the basement had been put into operation, construction proceeded rather slowly, for the walls were only about twenty feet high by early 1843. Ironically, it was Smith's assassination by Illinois militia on 27 June 1844 which assured the building's completion. Realizing that their forced departure from Nauvoo was imminent, the Mormons under the leadership of Brigham Young feverishly labored on the structure. Though all knew that the temple was to be shortly abandoned, they were unwilling to leave it undedicated, for, as will be seen, the dedication of the building was to be a most important event in the development of Mormon doctrine. A recent arrival from the east described the situation as follows:

> I have been to view the Temple. It is a splendid building. The top stone was laid with Praises and Hosannas the morning before I arrived [in late May 1845]. . . . The roof is partly on. It never went so fast before. Half has been built since Joseph was killed.[19]

In late July of that year, "the Temple progresses finely; the roof is nearly shingled; the framework of [the] steeple is nearly as high from the roof up as the body of the Temple."[20] The building was evidently felt to have been completed in all its essentials by 1 May 1846, when the official dedication took place.

The most intriguing aspect of the Nauvoo temple was certainly the new order which it displayed—the first appearance of an architectural symbolism with a basis in Mormon theology. Nowhere in the journals does Smith offer an explanation of precisely what this order was supposed to mean, but the answer is provided in a revelation which he received in February 1832, a revelation concerning the resurrection and those who shall be eternally rewarded. Now that his followers had been organized into a tightly structured hierarchical system through which one could progress to positions of leadership and authority, Smith extended this concept to the world beyond, in order to provide fairly for rewards and punishments which were merited by conduct during one's earthly life. The revelation divided heaven itself into levels of attainment, the highest of course being reserved for the keepers of the covenant of the Latter-day Saints:

> These are they whose bodies are celestial, whose glory is that of the sun, even the glory of God, the highest of all, whose glory the sun of the firmament is written of as being typical.
>
> And again, we saw the terrestrial world, and behold and lo,

these are they who are of the terrestrial, whose glory differs from that of the church of the Firstborn who have received the fulness of the Father, even as that of the moon differs from the sun in the firmament.

Behold, these are they who die without the law. . . .

And again, we saw the glory of the telestial, which glory is that of the lesser, even as the glory of the stars differs from that of the glory of the moon in the firmament. These are they who received not the Gospel of Christ. . . .[21]

These three graded levels of heavenly glory, the celestial, terrestrial, and telestial, with their assigned symbols of sun, moon, and stars, clarified and implemented the words of St. Paul in I Corinthians 15:40. St. Paul refers to degrees of glory (except for the telestial, which Smith added himself) but does not associate each state of glory with a specific heavenly body. The symbols on the new architectural order of the Nauvoo temple thus indicated the purpose of the building—the gaining of one of the kingdoms of heaven. Smith's followers working on the temple believed, as Josiah Quincy reported, that Smith had seen the sun, moon, and stars in a vision, though his secretary, Mr. Halkett, rather uncharitably compared the blazing sun faces of the capitals to public-house signs. Each capital was "in the form of a head surrounded by rays of light representing the rising sun; two hands holding trumpets, prototypes of doomsday,"[22] surmounted it, everything carved in high relief, the face with slightly puckered lips and a strangely cross-eyed expression. The crescent moons serving as pilaster bases also had carved features—the outlines of a face in profile—facing the ground (only traces of these are visible in the remaining stones, see figure 27).

The sun seen in conjunction with trumpets had appeared on New England gravestones of the eighteenth century to symbolize the morn of the Judgment Day, and the sun, moon, and stars appearing together on a single stone had also occurred, though no precise explanation of their funerary symbolism has been offered. Was the symbolism the result of memories which Smith may have had of such grave markers from his early youth in New England? Perhaps, but Smith's inspiration is more easily traceable to his association with a new institution.

On 15 March 1842 a Masonic lodge was installed at Nauvoo, following the granting of a dispensation by the Grand Master of Illinois in October 1841. This was not the first time that Smith had come into contact with Freemasonry in one way or another. In the late 1820s the Burned-over District was the scene of violent anti-Masonic outbursts after the abduction and supposed assassination of William Morgan, who had been about to reveal Masonic secrets. Masonry was decried as a threat to democracy and members of the organization were ousted from political office, while anti-Masonic meetings parodied the cer-

21. *Doctrine and Covenants* 66: 70–85. Smith seemed to want to provide for all honorable men to rise to at least one of these levels. The only people consigned to hell would be liars, sorcerers, adulterers, and whoremongers.

22. Henry Lewis, *The Valley of the Mississippi, Illustrated* [1854], trans. by A. Hermina Poatgieter, ed. by B. L. Heilbroner (St. Paul, 1967), p. 246.

23. Smith, *History of the Church*, VI, p. 608.

24. Robert Bruce
Flanders, *Nauvoo,
Kingdom on the
Mississippi* (Ur-
bana, 1965), p. 271.

monies before appreciatively hostile audiences throughout western New York. The furor over the Morgan case found its way into the Book of Mormon, which Smith was composing at precisely this time, for he introduced into the text a secret and insidious society whose rituals, oaths, and murderous intentions ultimately helped to precipitate the fratricidal Indian war.

The Book of Mormon's denunciations notwithstanding, Smith was eager to bring Freemasonry into Nauvoo, for by 1841 the controversy had subsided and Masonry was again socially respectable. Since Smith very much wanted to extend the influence of the Saints in Illinois politics, organizing a lodge seemed expedient. Most of the leading Mormons joined the lodge, so rapidly, in fact, that Freemasonry actually became an issue of conflict between Mormon and non-Mormon due to the speed with which Mormons passed through the ranks of the society. Smith became a Master Mason, the highest degree in the organization, the day after the lodge was installed, and within six months the Nauvoo lodge had two hundred eighty-six candidates, more than the total membership in the rest of the state.

Very soon the Prophet's fascination with the Masonic ceremonies began to make itself felt in religious matters. Only a few weeks after the lodge was organized Smith preached a sermon on the "keys of the kingdom," certain "signs and words by which false spirits and personages may be detected from true, which cannot be revealed to the Elders till the Temple is completed."[23] In private to some of his closest associates he gave instructions regarding the ancient order of things, the endowments and giving of keys. This order to which he initiated the men was designed to be performed in the temple and was to remain secret. After washing and anointing, the participants were dressed in a robe decorated with the Masonic square and compass on the breast, were sworn to secrecy, and then watched a drama depicting the creation and the fall, with Smith taking the role of God. Each man was told passwords, instructed in various grips and handshakes, and given a secret name by which he would be known in the kingdom of heaven. Rumors of this new ritual began to leak out (for the time being, the rites took place in the room over Smith's store), and by 1843 people "knew of the existence of a secret group of Saints, including women, called the 'Holy Order' whose private rites included symbolic reenactment of the Garden of Eden."[24]

The Masonic ritual would have appealed immediately to Smith, for it was concerned with exactly those Old Testament ideas which he had increasingly been incorporating into his religion. The Freemasons claimed that their society had originated in Biblical times, and its initiation ceremonies and mythology are centered around the architect Hiram Abiff, whom Solomon supposedly employed to build his temple. Freemasonry was attractive not only because of its constant references to the temple of Solomon, but because of its idea of progressive ad-

vancement in rank to be gained through proper performance of prescribed activities, a parallel with Mormonism's three levels of glory
which must have been at once apparent. The Masonic ritual was altered and "purified" by Smith to become one of greater religious significance; he substituted the story of Adam and Eve for that of Hiram
Abiff, while retaining the language and gestures. This became, along
with baptism, one of the things which had to be done to gain entrance
to the kingdom of heaven. The creation story meshed with the Edenic
aims of the Saints and bolstered the Adamic mythology which Smith
had been developing since writing the *Book of Mormon*. Equally significantly, it provided for the inclusion of women in the ceremonies,
giving them a greater, though distinctly subordinate, role in the activities of the church.

The new order of the Nauvoo temple, which appeared in abbreviated
form on the first of Weeks's drawings from 1842, bears a startling resemblance to some very prominent Masonic symbols which figure
in the ritual and are illustrated in Masonic handbooks (freely available throughout the nineteenth century). The three most important
Masonic emblems are the Bible, the compass, and the square, the
"three great lights" of Freemasonry—the Bible signifying God, the
square the master of the lodge, and the compass the craft of masonry.
These are accompanied by the "three lesser lights," the sun, moon,
and stars, which are symbols of officials in the lodge and also have
moral messages. Smith simply appropriated those Masonic elements
which were applicable to Mormonism, using the three lesser lights,
probably seen in illustrations (figure 33), to symbolize the three degrees of heavenly glory. The Weeks drawings show the gradual working out of this symbolism to include all three heavenly bodies.

At Nauvoo the temple became truly differentiated from the church.
Masonry added a new dimension to Mormon worship—it became
ritualistic and also secret, so that the temple was no longer a congregational center of town activity. The temple became a place set apart, like
a Masonic lodge, to be used only by those whom church authorities
had initiated into something great and mysterious. At Nauvoo Smith
began to refer to the temple as a "Holy of Holies" in the Solomonic
sense. The performance of the ritual took place in the western attic of
the temple, in the rectangular pediment area which was separated into
three chambers by curtains; the left side was for the women's rites and
the right side for the men. This may have been why the triangular
pediment of William Weeks's earlier plans was abandoned. Though
Smith was dead before the temple was far enough along to accommodate these ceremonies, they were inaugurated by Brigham Young in
December 1845, and as many Saints as possible received their endowments before leaving for the west. How the ritual would have affected the use of the temple had the Saints remained in Nauvoo is not
certain. There is no indication that Smith intended for the rituals to be

33. Frontispiece of James Hardie's The New Free-Mason's Monitor, *1818*

34. Masonic hall, Nauvoo

35. *Masonic hall at Nauvoo, as reconstructed by James Bilderback*

made public once the temple was completed, but if they remained clandestine there would have been some difficulty keeping the meeting halls open for general worship while prohibiting access to the basement and attic. In all likelihood the temple would have been closed to outsiders as the temples in Utah would be.

Joseph Smith did not lose interest in the Masonic lodge after he had adapted its format for his own use, and he continued to take an active interest in Masonic proceedings. In 1842 the cornerstone of a Masonic hall was laid, the first hall built specifically to house a lodge in the state of Illinois, and, as Smith boasted, the largest and finest. It was finished and dedicated in 1844, despite the revocation of the charter of the Nauvoo lodge by the Grand Lodge of Illinois because of improper proceedings, and was used not only for Masonic functions but for the performance of some temple ordinances.[25] This hall is still standing in mutilated condition (figure 34), having been converted from a three-story building to a two-story house. Fortunately, the inhabitant of the house in 1937 had as a young man assisted in its remodeling and was able to reconstruct its original appearance (figure 35) and provide a detailed description of the interior. Its architect has not been determined, though William Weeks is certainly a possibility. The facade of this structure is curiously similar to that of the Salt Lake City temple and may indeed be a transitional building between Nauvoo and the Utah temples. The tripartite division, with doors set back between buttress-like pilaster strips is similar to the recessing of the doors between the towers of the Salt Lake City temple. In proportion the building assumes greater verticality and the large keystones on the third-story window surrounds also figure prominently on the Salt Lake City temple. A fragment of a drawing for another version of the Masonic hall (figure 36), similar in style to the draftsmanship of the temple drawings, is still Greek Revival, but its bizarre pediment decoration is the Masonic all-seeing eye, a symbol which reappears in Salt Lake.

The Mormons at Nauvoo were obviously very familiar with Masonic symbolism and procedure, for the Nauvoo Masonic hall carefully followed the specifications for a correctly constructed Masonic building. There were no windows on the north side, since Freemasonry believed the north to be the direction of darkness, having slightly sinister connotations, and the front of the building faced towards the east, the direction of the rising sun. Significantly, the orientation of the building was a practice followed consistently in all the temples built in Utah—after the encounter with Freemasonry—while at Kirtland and Nauvoo, both planned before, this was not a consideration. Nauvoo of course faced west, towards the river. Kirtland faces east, but does not exhibit the relationship between exterior and interior seen in the Utah buildings. In Utah the facade facing east was symbolic of the more important priesthood, the Melchizedek, and the eastern end of the interior halls belonged to the same priesthood. But at Kirtland, though the

25. Fawn Brodie, *No Man Knows My History*, p. 282, note.

36. Fragment of a drawing for the Nauvoo Masonic hall

facade is towards the east, the arrangement of pulpits is reversed—the Melchizedek pulpits are in the western end, where the pulpit would normally be found in a Protestant church. The eastern end of the building thus does not seem to have had any significance until the Mormons realized that it was given special importance by the Freemasons.

The years 1841–1845 transformed Mormonism into a religion whose beliefs comprised many varied elements culled from a number of sources. By 1844 Joseph Smith had fashioned these bits and pieces into a finished product almost unrecognizable from the pre-Nauvoo church. In the 1830s and 1840s, Smith, largely an untutored man, had continued to educate himself through reading and study of secular texts as well as the Bible. He began to speculate about the nature of matter, under the influence of Thomas Dick's *Philosophy of a Future State*, a rhetorical hodgepodge which combined eighteenth-century optimism about the progress of mankind with scientific theories, millennial Christianity, and materialist philosophy, all used to prove the existence of an afterlife. Smith became convinced that it was not possible for matter to be created out of nothing, that it must already exist in some form. Furthermore, since nothing can exist which is not matter, what the Bible refers to as "spirit" must also be some kind of matter. The Book of Abraham, composed while the Saints were at Kirtland but not published until 1842, represents Smith's attempt to come to terms with the new science of astronomy and the materialist theories which Dick's work had opened up to him. Correcting the account of creation found in the Bible, the book stated in the words of Abraham, whom Smith presented as an astronomer, that the earth had been organized out of previously existing matter and that the stars were peopled by "spirit" beings of various degrees of intelligence—ideas found in *Philosophy of a Future State*.

Revelations received at Nauvoo decreed that the spirit is matter, but purer matter than that seen on earth, and that God himself is of flesh and blood. (Since God was material, the corollary was that God and Christ must be two individual personages.) When one is born, then, this is not an act of creation, but an embodiment of a spirit in earthly form so that it can fulfill the ritual necessary for eternal salvation after death. This theory of matter had other interesting ramifications, for if, as Dick believed and Smith now professed, matter was indestructible, the spirit must also possess bodily form in the resurrected state. This offered the promise of an afterlife of material existence similar to one's existence on earth and for the maintenance of relationships which had been established on earth in the heavenly kingdoms, in particular baptism and marriage, which were now interpreted as binding for not just earthly time, but for all of eternity.

One of the most radical of the revelations which were to follow one

26. Flanders,
Nauvoo, p. 267.

another in rapid succession was delivered in July 1843. Not only, the Lord said, was He of bodily substance, but He is an exalted man who had once had an earthly form like all men. If the new order of ritual which Smith was about to introduce to the Nauvoo community were to be observed, the revelation promised that men could also become gods, to reign over a world (one of the stars or planets) as God reigns over our own. Smith believed that he had found a Biblical justification for this doctrine of the plurality of gods (the Book of Abraham had already stated that "the Gods" had organized the earth). In studying Hebrew he had realized that the Hebrew word for God, "elohim," is actually the plural form of the word god and concluded from this that when the Old Testament referred to God, the correct translation should be "Gods."

Temple ritual, as a consequence of all these new doctrines, took on an overwhelming importance in the Mormon theological system. It was no longer sufficient to live according to the precepts of the Bible alone, but the rewards which were to come with the fulfillment of very specific and carefully defined rites were staggering. It is no wonder, then, that the temple, the only place where these ceremonies could take place properly, played such a significant part in Mormon life for the rest of the century.

Even as he was revealing these doctrines to his flock, Smith kept secret the most explosive of all and one which he had apparently been considering for some time. This was the doctrine of celestial marriage, known mistakenly to non-Mormons, as simple polygamy. The orthodox Mormon view is that Smith received a revelation about celestial marriage and polygamy while the Saints were still at Kirtland, where his interest in new possibilities in the marital relationship had been stimulated by reading about the polygamous marriages of the Hebrew prophets. Smith always publicly denied that he or any of his associates practiced polygamy, and it was only in 1852 that Brigham Young published in Salt Lake City the text of what he claimed to be the original revelation given to Smith on 12 July 1843. There is ample evidence that the doctrine of celestial marriage had been put forth in practice as well as theory at least by 1844 and that Smith, Young, and other important Saints had taken plural wives at Nauvoo. Celestial marriage was more complex than the connubial experiments of the Perfectionist colonies in New York; the doctrine held that "marriage, as well as other family relationships, was eternal in duration when properly solemnized or 'sealed' in special Mormon rites. . . . Since a man whose wife had died often remarried, in the life to come both would be his wives. It was but a simple and logical step to forsake monogamy in this life in favor of 'plurality.'"[26] A man could be married to one or several wives in two ways, either for time, which involved consummation of the marriage on earth, or for eternity, which *could* mean that the marriage was consummated but did not necessarily mean this. A celestial marriage simply meant that a woman would be married to a particular man in the afterlife.

For a man polygamy and celestial marriage were a way of building up the population of his heavenly kingdom, but for the woman a proper temple marriage was even more important. As far as the levels of heavenly glory were concerned, the woman was not an independent agent. She could rise only to the level that her husband did and was able to share vicariously in his glory. Thus to enjoy any kind of bliss in the afterlife, she had to be married, at least for eternity if not for time. As George Laub, a resident of Nauvoo in 1844, understood the new order of things, women

> must have the husband by their side and he is to rule over them and receav[e] the washing and anointing and the Sealing power for them to be Sealed together . . . and these are certain keys and words that do not belong to the woman . . . then he shall teach the woman and preside over all the family of his redeemed. This will make a man to be a God to his family for this is the order and organisation of heaven.[27]

27. Diary of George Laub, reporting on a sermon by Heber Kimball on resurrection, given 29 December, 1844, manuscript in the Church Historian's Office, Salt Lake City.

Thus when Brigham Young initiated the new rites in the temple in December 1845, they consisted of a number of elements—baptism and baptism for the dead (which had been performed in the basement for several years), the giving of endowments and keys of the kingdom through the Mormon-Masonic ritual of the reenactment of the creation and expulsion in the temple attic, and the sealings and plural marriages, also performed in the attic. Although these goings-on in Nauvoo were certainly an aberration on the American scene, there are general similarities between the increasingly ritualized nature of Mormonism and movements in traditional Christianity, such as the formation of the Ecclesiological Society in the east, a manifestation of the mid-nineteenth century's desire for greater formalism in worship and more sense of continuity with the early history of Christianity. In a strange way, Smith was attempting the same thing at Nauvoo.

It might seem that with all these accretions Mormonism had lost touch with its original millennialist intentions, but this was not the case. Throughout the Nauvoo period the energy of the Latter-day Saints remained directed towards the establishment of Zion on earth, and the new ritual was part of what had to be done in preparation for the millennium. Constructing the temple and increasing the population and prosperity of Nauvoo were regarded as part of the work of building up the kingdom, and with the success of the settlement in Illinois, Smith's expectations for the Saints began to expand. The New Jerusalem was to be more than just the Mormon city—at Nauvoo he began to refer to the whole of America as Zion, again in the literal sense. Smith saw himself and the Saints as God's instruments in the

28. Klaus J. Hansen, *Quest for Empire*, p. 54.

saving of the United States government from corruption and the means whereby an actual political kingdom of God would be set up to rule the world when Christ came to inaugurate the last and greatest age in the history of the world.

Joseph Smith had received a revelation about this political kingdom in 1842, but he did not move to implement it until 1844 and then only with the utmost secrecy. The Nauvoo Legion was already deemed by the Mormon populace the instrument by which the kingdom was to be established, but in addition, Smith formed a secret governing body of his most trusted colleagues, called the Council of Fifty, to set up the machinery of government and be ready to assume rule of the world when Christ appeared. This body was separate from the government of the church, and, theoretically at least, it was possible for non-Mormons to be members, though in fact it was comprised of the Mormon hierarchy. Since Smith took literally the scriptural dictum that Christ would rule as king of the earth, the function of the Council of Fifty during the millennium would be primarily to administer the laws of the kingdom of God. But the Council's function until this time would also be executive, since until the arrival of Christ the Prophet was to be his envoy. With the authority of his secret council behind him, Smith sent out ambassadors to explore the possibility of recognition of the kingdom of God by foreign powers, while announcing himself as a candidate for president of the United States in 1844.

A portion of the laws of the kingdom referred to the social order—the established marital form was to be polygamy, so to reside in Christ's millennial realm it was required that a man take more than one wife. As Klaus Hansen explains:

> The political kingdom, of course, did not depend upon polygamy for its survival, but plural marriage could only be practiced in ethical and moral terms within the kingdom. . . . It could also serve as a rallying point and symbol of identification for a people who, in spite of all the special qualities of their faith, shared most of the basic cultural characteristics of their fellow Americans. More than anything else, polygamy could stamp these folk as a "peculiar people" and thus aid them in establishing a national identity for the kingdom of God.[28]

Polygamy was certainly one of the reasons why, even during his campaign for the presidency, Smith delegated the Council of Fifty to seek out a new location for the kingdom of God, for a Mormon polygamous empire had no hopes of surviving in Illinois—it must isolate itself and gain strength before trying to overcome the kingdoms of the world. He had been eyeing the western states with a view towards expansion into these unpopulated areas and as early as 1842 had predicted that the Mormons would eventually migrate west.

The Saints were experiencing other difficulties unrelated to their peculiar marital practices (which, in spite of official secrecy, were well known around Nauvoo). They had been playing a dangerous game of brinkmanship with the political parties in Illinois. Smith gave both parties a potential weapon to use against the Mormons by announcing that the Saints would vote in a block for whichever party appeared to be most pro-Mormon in its policies. Initially this led to a rash of promises by candidates, but the eventual outcome was that both parties felt themselves betrayed by the Mormons, who they believed were undemocratically making deals with the opposing party and switching promised votes at the last moment. The neighboring towns in addition resented the political supremacy of Nauvoo and the special privileges given to it by its charter. The final incident which led to the fall of Nauvoo came from within the city itself, however. A group of renegade Mormons had set up a printing press and had published one issue of the Nauvoo *Expositor*, whose express purpose was to reveal the secret practices going on in the church and expose Smith's imperial aspirations. In his haste to stop the group, Smith overstepped the lines of practices which the gentiles were willing to tolerate and ordered the press smashed and all copies of the paper destroyed. Smith and his brother voluntarily surrendered to the militia for trial and were assassinated by a mob in the jail at Carthage, Illinois, on 27 June 1844.

Leadership of the church was almost immediately assumed by Brigham Young, the head of the Twelve Apostles. Though preparations began, the move west was not undertaken immediately, for when Smith was killed the walls of the temple were only halfway up, and Young now assigned top priority to the completion of the building. It was imperative that the temple be dedicated before being abandoned. When he had released the revelation about baptism for the dead, Smith had set an unspecified time limit by which the building had to be completed or else the Lord would take away his blessings from the Saints. This threat had been used to spur the inhabitants to labor harder on the temple and contribute money. Completing the temple was also an incentive to those who had not yet joined the main community of Saints to hasten to the gathering, for they were told that the temple was the only place where they could receive their endowments. To leave the temple unfinished and the people unendowed would have been a tragedy. By completing it, Young brought the Nauvoo period to a definitive end and assured those who were about to leave for unknown hardships that their destiny at Nauvoo had been fulfilled. The destruction of the temple by arsonists confirmed in the minds of the Mormons the perfidy of the gentiles, and it became a symbol of their isolation from American society.

Architecturally the temple was unique on the western frontier, though its value derived more from what it said about those who

29. Thomas G. Ford,
A History of Illinois
(Chicago, 1854), p.
404.

erected it than from its intrinsic architectural merits. Thomas Ford, the governor of Illinois during the stay of the Mormons, assessed the temple thus:

> It has been said that the church architecture of a sect indicates the genius and spirit of its religion. The grand and solemn structures of the Catholics point to the towering hierarchy, and imposing ceremonies of the church; the low and broad meeting-houses of the Methodists formerly shadowed forth their abhorence of gaudy decoration. . . . If the genius of Mormonism were tried by this test, as exhibited in the temple, we could only pronounce that it was a piece of patchwork, variable, strange, and incongruous.[29]

What Ford neglected to note was that the Nauvoo temple was a highly original structure, its awkwardness due in part to the attempt to create an architectural identity for a new people. The exterior of the temple was in actuality not truly indicative of what Mormonism had become by the time the Saints left the city, for the ritual was formulated while the building was going up, and the possible consequences of these changes, with the exception of the new order, could not be incorporated into the building. Smith and Weeks did not regard the building as belonging outside the tradition of American architecture, for the temple certainly manifests a desire to keep pace with contemporary trends. The temple represents, rather, an effort to compete with the architecture of the non-Mormon world on its own terms while only just beginning to signify the distinctiveness of the creed to which it belonged.

Chapter 5

Salt Lake City

One of the first actions taken by Brigham Young after the arrival of the Saints in the valley of the Great Salt Lake in 1847 was the dedication of a plot of land for the construction of a temple. Young had left Nauvoo fully intending to erect a temple somewhere in the Great Basin, for the Mormons had decided (after eliminating Texas, California, and Oregon as possibilities because of their already sizeable populations) that this was to be their final destination. For the time being, the dedication was only a symbolic gesture, survival dictating that work on the building be postponed until the settlement had gained a foothold. The harshness of the first winters and the lack of food and supplies delayed any planning or construction until several years later. In 1851 a vote was taken at the Seventies Conference to begin work, financed by tithing. Truman O. Angell was named architect of public buildings and placed in charge of the project.

Truman Osborn Angell had been a loyal Latter-day Saint almost since the founding of the church. He was born in 1810 in North Providence, Rhode Island, where at age seventeen he "commenced learning the carpenters and joiners trade, under the instruction of a man in the neighborhood of my father's house, and continued with him until I was twenty."[1] He joined the Mormons after moving to Genesee County, New York, at age twenty-three. Though there are no details of his early life, it can be assumed that he continued to practice his trade, for when he went to Kirtland in 1835, he "immediately commenced working upon the house of the Lord and continued until its dedication."[2] Angell went to Missouri for a year after the Kirtland Bank debacle, spent two years on a farm near Quincy, Illinois, and then moved to Nauvoo, working under William Weeks as first foreman on the temple until the lower story was ready for use. After Weeks left, Angell took over as supervisor of construction until the building was completed, then headed west to join the rest of the Saints in Utah.

As the man who knew the most about temple building after Weeks, Angell was the natural choice to assume the responsibility of the official architect's position. Even so, he found his new duties difficult:

1. Autobiography of Truman O. Angell, manuscript in the Church Historian's Office, Salt Lake City.
2. *Ibid*.

3. A Journal Kept by
Truman O. Angell,
entry for 15 De-
cember, 1851,
manuscript in the
Church Historian's
Office.

Soon business increased . . . the President wished me to devote
my time to making out designs and plans and see that they were
executed, saying I need not work further. This to some may seem
easy but I have always been since my manhood a hard working
carpenter and joiner with my own hands, but it is a trifle to labour
with one's own hands [compared] to the labour of the mind.[3]

Angell struggled with the temple plans for three years, until Young
sent him to Europe in 1856 to gain greater knowledge of architectural
styles and designs, so as to be better qualified to work on the temple
and other buildings which the Saints intended to erect. This trip appears to have been Angell's first real contact with architecture, and he
remained singularly unimpressed by most of what he saw during his
travels in England and France. (In his journal, he noted that the new
Houses of Parliament "was burdened with ornaments till it became
sickening." Westminster Abbey "exhibited the genius of men, but
there was something about it very inanimate.") The major purpose of
the trip in fact was to study the European factory system with an eye to
potential adoption in Utah. Angell's contact with architecture in
Europe did not affect the Salt Lake temple, however, since the plans
had been completed before he left the United States and he made no
significant changes after his return.

On 6 April 1853, the anniversary of the church's founding, the cornerstone of the temple had been laid, and by June 1855 the foundation
of red sandstone was finished—sixteen feet deep so as to secure the
building against mountain floods, and sixteen feet wide at the base.
Work continued intermittently, dependent upon vicissitudes of harvest
and finance, and interrupted in 1857 by the so-called Mormon War,
when the incursion of federal troops brought construction to a halt for
three years. The battlements were finished in 1886 and the capstone
laid on 6 April 1892, the completed building rising to a height of 167½
feet on the side walls and 210 feet to the top of the highest tower on the
east, which was surmounted by a gilded statue of the angel Moroni.
The temple was dedicated a year later, exactly forty years after it was
begun.

Angell's journals reveal a man of logical, simple thoughts who was
intent upon solving problems presented to him and working to the best
of his ability. With only a minimal education, he found writing burden-
some; most of the journal entries are brief summaries of the day's
work, which included drawing up plans for a sugar-beet factory and a
house for Brigham Young as well as the temple. The journals are almost more interesting in their omission than in their actual content,
for there is scant mention of anything but matters of practicality. Curiously he never once mentions the style of the Salt Lake City temple,
nor any ideas he might have had about it, and the closest he comes to
assessing his role in the design is to say that the finishing touches of

the towers are "quite original." This leads to the unavoidable conclusion that, his position as official church architect notwithstanding, Angell's contribution to the creation of the Salt Lake City temple was in the areas of drafting and construction.

Brigham Young did have definite ideas about what the temple should be. It is to the church president that the creation of the Utah style must be attributed, and one must look beyond his public dissembling about his role as revelator in architectural matters. Young preferred to minimize the part which revelation played in the life of the Saints, and at the groundbreaking ceremonies said that a revelation was not necessary to know that a temple was needed in Salt Lake City:

> Brother Joseph often remarked that a revelation was no more necessary to build a Temple than a dwelling house; if a man knew he needed a kitchen, a bedroom, a parlor, etc., he needed no revelation to inform him of the fact; and I and my brethren around me know what is wanting in a Temple, having received all the ordinances therein.[4]

He agreed, however, that if a revelation was desired, he could get one. At the laying of the cornerstone he tantalized his listeners by disclosing that he had in fact had a revelation five years earlier that the temple would have six towers, but admonished them to wait until it was finished to see what the building would look like.

William Ward, Angell's assistant, stated many years afterwards that President Young had come into the architect's office and had drawn a sketch of how he proposed the temple to look and that Angell had worked from this sketch in drawing up the plans. As they were completed he took them to the president for his approval.[5] Angell's journals and correspondence also establish that the plans were the product of only himself and Brigham Young. The church architect never mentioned anyone else in connection with the progress of the plans and in some cases stated explicitly that certain ideas were given to him by the church leader. Young himself never spoke much about the temple to anyone (Ward said in 1892 that he did not recall any discussion of style between Young and Angell), but some valuable information can be gleaned from his addresses delivered in Salt Lake City in the 1850s and 1860s.

In 1851 the president reported to the people that the church conference had decided that the temple was to be built of the best material available in America—within reason, for Young reminded his congregation that nothing of gold or silver could rise in Salt Lake City without something more in the tithing boxes than "old half-dead stinking cows, and old broken kneed horses. . . ."[6] As for himself, Young preferred a surprisingly mundane material, adobe. Matters of practicality entered into this choice, for there was almost no wood in the valley and adobe was cheap and could be quickly manufactured. Most of the

4. *Deseret News Weekly*, 14 February, 1853.
5. *Deseret News*, 15 April, 1892.
6. *Journal of Discourses by Brigham Young, His Two Counsellors, The Twelve Apostles, and Others*, 26 vols. (Liverpool, 1854–1886) 4th reprint, I (1854), p. 218.

7. *Journal of Discourses*, I, (1854), p. 218.
8. For example in *Journal of Discourses*, X (1865), p. 254, Young is reported to have said, "I want to see the Temple built in a manner that it will endure through the Millennium." Also *Journal of Discourses*, XI (1867), p. 372.

houses in the town in the 1850s were made out of adobe bricks. However his argument for the use of adobe rather than sandstone or limestone was founded upon a more important consideration, the need for permanence. Offering a "chemical argument" for his choice, Young compared adobe to the stone available in the Wasatch mountains east of Salt Lake City. "If you take this clay . . . and mix it with these pebble rocks, and make adobies of the compound, it will petrify in the wall and become a solid rock in five hundred years . . . while the other materials I have mentioned will have decomposed, and gone back to their native elements." [7]

Young's desire that the building last a long time is easy enough to fathom. The temple was not to stand simply until it needed replacing by a larger or newer building, it was being constructed for the millennium and *had* to be sturdy—as long-lived as the pyramids of Egypt to which he compared it and which he believed had also been constructed of adobe. In succeeding years Young stated several times that he wanted the Salt Lake City temple to stand for a thousand years. [8] Small wonder, then, that stylistic considerations (style in this case connoting fashion or vogue) carried so little weight with the Mormons, and there was no argument carried on among church authorities about this question. Their temple was to be a structure which stood outside of time and marked the end of human history with its transient and ephemeral styles. Interestingly in the same speech where he recommended adobe as a building material, Young compared the projected temple with the United States Capitol, built in 1812 but already needing repairs, its stone columns decayed like those of the ancient world. How different from the building to be put up by the government of God, which would endure while the kingdoms of this world degenerated! Already Young had perhaps repudiated neoclassicism as inappropriate for Mormon architecture.

Inelegant and ultimately as impractical as it was, the adobe proposal was adopted. Angell's first drawing, a ground plan of the basement dated 1853 (figure 37), indicates that the exterior wall was to have been constructed of mud, straw, and pebbles. The adobe building was apparently never started, for it was demonstrated that the foundations could not support a high wall. Thereupon granite was substituted. The great value placed upon durability is shown by the Mormons' selection of granite, the hardest local stone, as a substitute, even though it had to be hauled from the mountains nineteen miles away, and by the tremendous thickness of the walls at their base—eight feet of solid rock.

The disposition of the basement rooms as shown on the 1853 plan was similar to Nauvoo, with a large oval font in the center and small rooms at the sides, though the rooms at either end now occupied the entire width of the basement. The rooms north and south of the font were intended for donning the ritual robes and for the preliminary

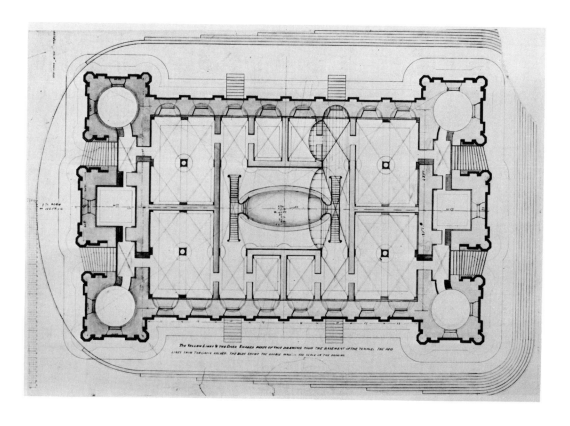

37. Angell's drawing of the ground plan of the Salt Lake temple, 1853

9. Richard Burton,
*The City of the
Saints* [1861], ed. by
Fawn M. Brodie
(New York, 1963),
p. 244.

washings and anointings. The larger chambers were to be for the giving of endowments during the dramatic representation of the creation story, thus concentrating the entire ritual in the basement. Throughout the forty years of construction the ritual instituted at Nauvoo was of course not set aside. In another example of the interchangeability with which religious and civic buildings were regarded, the upper rooms of the state house were prepared to be used as endowment rooms, and the ritual commenced in February 1851. A special temporary building, Endowment House, was erected a few years later specifically for this function and continued to be used until the dedication of the temple.

Endowment House was the first sanctified Mormon building which was off limits for all those who were not participating in the ceremony. The cloak-and-dagger goings-on of Smith and his friends in Nauvoo became a sort of public secret in Utah. There had been no intention to close the Nauvoo temple to the general public, though it probably would have been closed once the new rites had been firmly incorporated into Mormon theology and practice. In Utah, however, secrecy became an accepted and formalized part of the system, an aspect which coexisted with public meetings of worship. Everyone, even gentiles, knew that a ritual was being practiced, though it was envisioned by outsiders as being wilder and more unusual than it actually was. Endowment House was not used for conferences and Sunday gatherings, but *only* for ritual—including polygamous marriages—which was transferred to the temple at its completion. (By 1893 the federal government had outlawed polygamy and the church had repudiated it; conventional marriages still take place in the temple.) It was here in Salt Lake City that the final transformation of the New England meetinghouse took place. During the process of constructing the temple, the Mormons were busily erecting the functional equivalent of churches, the tabernacles and ward chapels, to serve the devotional needs which Kirtland and Nauvoo would have accommodated. Thus by 1893 there were two separate categories of religious buildings, whereas in the east there had been but one.

The peripatetic Englishman Richard Burton, whose fascination with the unusual led him to most of the exotic areas of the world, described Endowment House as he saw it in 1860:

> In the extreme N.W. angle of the [temple] Block is the Endowment, here pronounced *On-dewment House*, separated from the Tabernacle by a high wooden paling. The building . . . is of adobe with a pent roof and four windows, one blocked up: the central and higher portion is flanked by two wings, smaller erections of the same shape . . . The two small wings are said to contain fonts for the two sexes, where baptism by total immersion is performed.[9]

38. Angell's drawing of the east facade of the Salt Lake temple, 1854

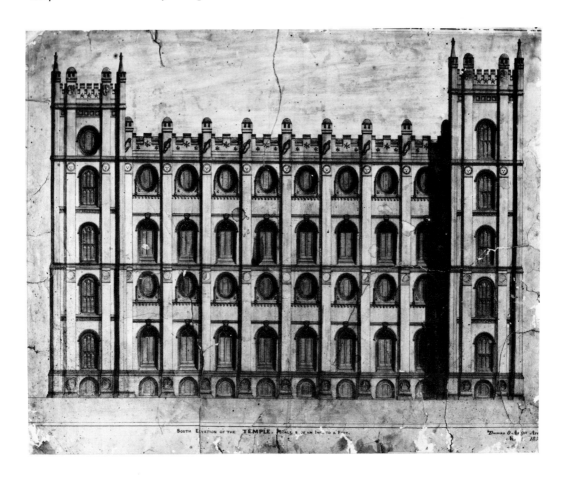

39. *Angell's drawing of the south elevation of the Salt Lake temple,*
1854

This description, and Burton's observation that "of late, as in the old Quaker meeting houses at Philadelphia, the brethren in the Tabernacle have been separated from the 'sistern,' . . ."[10] confirm that the Mormons were practicing sexual segregation at least by this time, if not earlier. The two entrances on the north and south sides of the basement plan certainly must have been to allow direct entry to the preparation rooms, with the women on the left and the men on the right. Since this separation was observed in the meetings held in the tabernacle, it is reasonable to suppose that the two sets of doors on the east and west facades of the temples were to allow access to the halls, with left and right distinctions being followed, the side which one entered being determined by whichever of the two priesthoods was going to preside.

Angell published a description of the temple in the *Deseret News* in 1854 after he had completed the elevations; this was revised and republished in 1874. Together with correspondence and the drawings themselves (figures 38 and 39) they provide an idea of the general appearance of this unique creation which was to be the temple. Perfectly symmetrical in plan, the total length was to be 168½ feet, and the width, including towers, 188½ feet, quite a bit more ambitious than Nauvoo. The interior of the temple has undergone considerable alteration since Angell drew up his plans, but in its original state it would have been very similar to the temple in Illinois. Each hall was to have the required double set of pulpits, and a mezzanine story above each hall was to have eight rooms on either side, presumably to serve as meeting rooms and offices. No information was given in the descriptions about the decoration of the interior, probably because the architect realized that it would be some time before any interior furnishings would be needed. Throughout the 1850s and 1860s Angell was working out the details of the interior, and there are many drawings of window frames, columns, and entablatures (see figures 59 and 60).

The two drawings of the exterior, both signed and dated March 1854 (figures 38 and 39), show the east facade elevation and the south flank. Along the sides, Angell substituted buttresses for pilasters but retained the four-story, eight-bay elevation of Nauvoo, even to the inclusion of the mezzanine windows, now elliptical rather than round as a concession to the greater verticality of the Gothic style. The basement windows give the impression of being another level of large windows cut off by their disappearance into the ground. The stories are carefully demarcated by string courses and by a decorative reduction of an arched corbel table below the mezzanine windows. Breaking in just at the level of the sill of the second story of large windows, the buttresses emphasize that in actuality the elevation has two major divisions which are then subdivided into sections of greater and lesser importance. This horizontal articulation of the stories negates to a significant extent the potential verticality of the Gothic, and it is clear that

10. *Ibid.* This tabernacle had two doors, as did many in the nineteenth century.

11. Carroll L. V. Meeks, "Romanesque Before Richardson in the United States," *Art Bulletin*, 35, 1 (1953): 17–33.
12. These changes were made in the 1880's by Truman Angell, Jr. Though the windows of the flanks and towers are now the same shape, there is still a distinction maintained by the inclusion of inset frames of lighter colored limestone in the tower windows.
13. Truman Angell to John Taylor, 29 April, 1886, letter in the Church Historian's Office, Salt Lake City.

the soaring, sublime effect which so delighted the proponents of the Gothic Revival for church architecture was not a factor in the planning of the Salt Lake City temple. Beneath the medieval veneer it is possible to detect the broad, classical proportions of Nauvoo, with a hint of a pedimented roof between the towers.

Three tiered spires now rise above roof level at either end, greatly increasing the visual complexity of the upper portion of the building. Angell planned for them to be built of wood, but in 1887 when construction reached the level of the battlements, it was decided that they should be of stone. The towers were not thought of as truly organic parts of the building, but as appurtenances to the functioning part of the structure and so were differentiated from the rest of the building by architectural devices. One would be hard put to describe exactly what is Gothic about the temple as it exists today aside from the battlements and buttresses. The large windows, if they are medieval at all, seem to belong to what Meeks has defined as the "round-arch style"[11] of the pre-Richardsonian romanesque, while the huge keystones connote some connection with the classical tradition. But in the 1854 drawings the windows of the towers all have Perpendicular Gothic tracery in them, and the two windows of the center tower are elaborated with an ogee arch molding. These are purposefully different from the windows of the flanks, which have simple shutters and no tracery. Moreover, the number and shapes of the tower windows are not consistent with the flanks, and the minor string courses which subdivide the sections of the towers do not align with those of the sides. The building as it was completed (figures 40 and 41) regularized the string courses so as to create a continuous line from tower to body at all levels where this was possible, making the building much more insistently uniform and at the same time destroying much of the subtle distinction between the symbolic and the operational parts of the temple.[12]

The Salt Lake City temple was the first Mormon temple to express externally the organization of the hierarchy into two priesthoods, the Aaronic and the Melchizedek, for each end of the temple belonged to one priesthood, and the towers were intended to be symbolic of the difference between the two. This distinction was communicated by height:

> The original design was to represent the greater priesthood with the east end, and the lesser with the west end, therefore the difference in height. With more mature reflection it was observed that the lesser priesthood depended entirely upon the greater, and it would be more strikingly typical with the windows left out, especially as their *only* object was for exterior appearance.[13]

The windows omitted were those intended for the top level of the western towers (compare figures 39 and 41), but even in the 1854 plans the lesser importance of the western end was indicated by placing a small

40. *East facade of the Salt Lake temple*

41. Salt Lake temple from the south

elliptical window there instead of a large round-arched window. The west center tower was to rise to a height of 194 feet at the top of the spire and the east would be 16 feet higher, a discrepancy which is not immediately noticeable, and when noticed hardly detracts from the overall symmetry of the temple.

Further divisions within the priesthoods were signified by increasing the number of towers at each end from one to three. When the first description of the temple was published in August 1854, the details of the spires had not yet been decided upon, and Angell consequently says nothing about them. But he explained in the 1874 version that each tower was to have twelve pinnacles, "emblemmatical of the First Presidency, Twelve Apostles, High Council, Bishops and their Counselors, etc."[14] Precisely what Angell meant by this is impossible to explain with the information now available, for he did not divulge whether there existed a one-to-one relationship between the pinnacles and offices of the church (thirty-six was the total number of pinnacles at each end, but there are not thirty-six offices in each priesthood). The organization of the church was so complex and interlocking that it is impossible to designate specifically what each element of the towers signified. The most logical explanation is William Ward's, that the eastern end symbolized the president and his counselors and the western end the presiding bishop and his two counselors. The triple towers divided into three parts also repeat the arrangement of the pulpits which were to stand at the ends of the interior halls.

To suppose that the battlement levels were somehow symbolic is not reading too much hidden meaning into the building, for most of the decoration did have an underlying message. Angell described some of the carved stones which were to adorn the exterior of the temple. At first these were to be carved of "freestone" and set into the adobe walls, but this was changed by 1854 to a low relief carved upon the granite. On the west center tower, a few feet below the crenellations, was the Big Dipper, pointing to the North Star (figures 42 and 43): "Moral, the lost may find themselves by the priesthood." Visible on the drawings are the by now familiar sun, moon, and stars. The sun, considerably smaller than at Nauvoo and with less pronounced features, is just below the castellations and shown full-face surrounded by small rays. The moon is represented in its phases just below the center string course, on what appears to be a "capital" of the buttress, with features shown only in its crescent phase, at the south-west corner. The phases begin at the center of the south side of the temple and move left around the building, ending with December again on the south side.[15] On the keystones of the arched windows and over the shutters can be seen the stars.

By this time these astronomical symbols were generally understood to signify the levels of glory. Even Benjamin Ferris, the despised secretary of the Territory of Utah during the winter of 1852–53, was aware

14. *Millennial Star*, 26 (1874).

15. A drawing in the Church Historian's Office signed by Truman Angell, Jr., shows the phases of the moon worked out for the year 1878. It is doubtful that the positions of the phases on the temple had any particular significance. Angell probably used 1878 because construction was approaching the level of the moonstones at about this time.

42. Central tower, west facade

43. Detail, showing the Big Dipper

16. Benjamin G. Ferris, *Utah and the Mormons* (New York, 1854), p. 44.
17. See *Millennial Star*, 26 (1874).
18. Wallace A. Raynor, *The Everlasting Spires* (Salt Lake City, 1965), p. 171.
19. Daniel 7:13–14.

that the sun, moon, and stars were the "three glories or degrees of salvation in store for all true Latter-day Saints."[16] This cosmology was elaborated upon by the addition, a few feet above ground level, of "earth stones," literally and figuratively the lowest level of symbolic stones. The explanation for these stones offered in 1874, but not before, was that "the Gospel has come for the whole earth."[17] Indeed the whole earth is there to be seen, for each stone was to depict a different aspect of the earth in rotation (figure 44). The spreading of the gospel over the entire earth must also have been understood as referring to the gathering and to one's subcelestial existence as well, the level from which one rose after proper performance of the basement rites to the glories signified by the higher symbolic stones.

Angell's plans also called for the inclusion of "cloud stones," with rays of light emanating from them, to be placed at the termination of each of the buttresses on the six towers. These now appear on the completed structure, but only on the front buttresses of the center tower of the eastern facade (figure 45). Raynor states that the cloud stones are meant to refer to the gospel light, "piercing through the clouds dispelling the clouds of superstition and error which had engulfed the world."[18] This may be so, but it is a meaning which these stones acquired *ex post facto* and is not corroborated by any primary sources. More in keeping with the interests of the Saints and the programmatic content of the stones described so far is the symbolic connotation which clouds carry in the Bible.

The cloud signifying the presence of the Lord—specifically, the coming of Christ—is a recurring motif of both Old and New Testaments and usually has millennial meaning. One of Daniel's dreams is a vision of the coming of the Messiah:

> I saw in the night visions, and, behold, one like the Son of man came with the clouds of heaven, and came to the Ancient of days, and they brought him near before him.
> And there was given him dominion, and glory, and a kingdom, that all people, nations, and languages should serve him: his dominion is an everlasting dominion, which shall not pass away, and his kingdom shall not be destroyed.[19]

Christ used the same symbol, in conjunction with other celestial motifs important to the Saints:

> And there shall be signs in the sun, and in the stars; and upon the earth distress of nations, with perplexity; the sea and waves roaring;
> Men's hearts failing them for fear, and for looking after those things which are coming on earth; for the powers of heaven shall be shaken.
> And they shall see the Son of man coming in a cloud with power and great glory.

44. Drawing for an earth stone

45. East facade, showing cloud stones

And when these things begin to come to pass, then look up, and lift your heads; for your redemption draweth nigh.[20]

Only four verses later occurs the passage which Smith had quoted to his friends at Nauvoo when predicting that the millennium would commence during their lifetime, "Verily I say unto you, This generation shall not pass away, till all be fulfilled."[21]

The cloud appears in the first chapter of the book of Revelation:

> Behold, he cometh with clouds; and every eye shall see him, and they also which pierced him; and all kindreds of the earth shall wail because of him. Even so, Amen.
>
> I am Alpha and Omega, the beginning and the ending, saith the Lord, which is, and was, and which is to come, the Almighty.[22]

The association of the clouds with the Second Coming is specifically made in a drawing of 1854, where hands holding trumpets emerge from the clouds, signifying the day of judgment (figure 46). Inscribed on the keystones of each of the windows in the center towers are the words, "I am Alpha and Omega." The clouds and the phrase lend the building a millennial meaning in keeping with Young's desire to have the temple endure for a thousand years, a meaning reinforced by the figure of the angel Moroni at the top of the eastern center tower, whose appearance to Smith in 1820 was believed by the Mormons to be the fulfillment of another scriptural passage, Revelation 14:6–7:

> And I saw another angel fly in the midst of heaven having the everlasting gospel to preach unto them that dwell on the earth, and to every nation, and kindred, and tongue, and people.
>
> Saying with a loud voice, Fear God, and give glory to Him; for the hour of his judgment is come; and worship him that made heaven, and earth, and the sea, and the fountains of water.

The facades of the temple can, in fact, be seen as a transposition of the promise of the book of Revelation into visual imagery, with the sun, moon, and stars pointing to the eternal rewards to be gained through the priesthood. The image of the eye carved into the inset molding of the higher window in the center towers—on the eastern end below the panel containing the dates of construction and the phrase "Holiness to the Lord," and at the west beneath the Big Dipper (figures 42, 43, and 47)—though a Masonic symbol, can be accommodated in this iconographical system of merited rewards in the hierarchies of the world to come. The all-seeing eye of God, "Whom Sun, Moon, and Stars obey, and under whose watchful care even comets perform their stupendous revolutions, pervades the inmost recesses of the human heart, and will reward us according to our merits."[23]

The last symbolic stone mentioned in Angell's descriptions is "Saturn and his rings," the most mysterious of all the symbols on the tem-

20. Luke 21:25–26.
21. Luke 21:32.
22. Revelation 1:7–8. Also, LDS hymn #88, with words by Parley P. Pratt, "now his chariot is the cloud."
23. Thomas Smith Webb, *Freemason's Monitor; or Illustrations of Masonry* (Salem, 1812), p. 72.

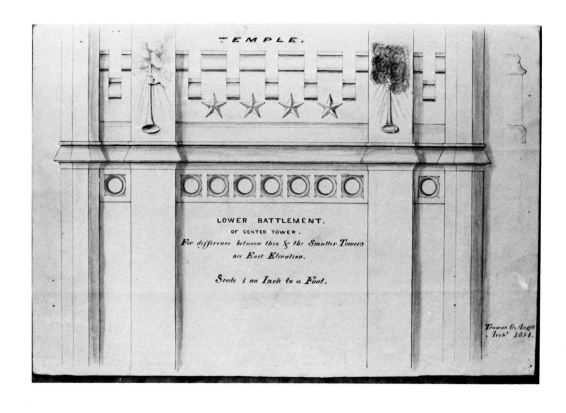

46. Drawing for the lower battlement of the center tower

47. Elevation of a window, showing all-seeing eye

24. Thomas Dick,
*Collected Works of
Thomas Dick*, 2
vols. (Philadelphia,
1843), I, p. 48.
25. *Ibid.*, p. 47.
26. *Ibid.*, p. 48–49.

ple. On the drawing of the side elevation, Saturn and the rings are
displayed prominently on the buttresses just above the sun stones,
showing very clearly that two rings surround the planet. The enigma
of these stones has to do with their lack of a discernible basis in Mormon theology. Saturn is never mentioned in the Bible or any of the
Mormon texts, Angell offers no explanation, and Brigham Young never
spoke or wrote about the planet. It may have had some private significance for the church president, but whatever meaning it had was
confused by 1893, when a special dedication souvenir issue of the
Contributor, published in Salt Lake City, identified the small band of
circular stones just below the battlements as representing Saturn,
even though Saturn as shown on Angell's drawings had long since
been eliminated from the design.

One source of speculation about Saturn to which Mormons appear to have had access was the philosophy of Thomas Dick (which
Joseph Smith had read while the Saints were at Kirtland). In his attempt to come to terms with the vastness of the universe and to recon-
cile the potentially shattering effect of eighteenth-century astronomical discoveries with Christian theology, Dick devoted much discussion
to his theory of the multiplicity of worlds, by which he endeavored to
incorporate the discovery of new planets and stars into his argument
that man's destiny was boundless. God, he argued, has given man the
ability to make inventions necessary to determine the size and dis-
tances of the planets. It must therefore have been his will that the
glories of the remote spaces of creation should be revealed to the inhabitants of the earth. A limitless universe proved for Dick the existence of an afterlife, or future state, where "amidst this boundless scene
of Divine Wisdom and Omnipotence, it is evident, that the soul might
expatiate in the full exercise of its energies, during ages numerous as
the drops of the ocean, without ever arriving at a boundary to interrupt
its excursions."[24] He speculated that the soul would be irresistibly
drawn to the furthest planets and stars, which "appear to be furnished
with every thing requisite for the accommodation of intellectual beings."[25] The soul would pass its time discovering the mysteries of
these inhabited worlds:

> Are all those vast globes peopled with inhabitants? are they con-
> nected together, under the government of God, as parts of one vast
> moral system? are their inhabitants pre moral intelligences . . . ?
> What are the gradations of rank or intellect which exist among
> them . . . ? Is this mighty expanse of creation to endure forever,
> and to receive new accessions to its population and grandeur,
> while eternity rolls on?[26]

Its striking appearance made Saturn especially fascinating to Dick,
and of all the planets he discusses, the most attention is given to this

one. Its stupendous size and luminous rings made it unthinkable that its creation could have been for any purpose other than to figure in some scheme of a divine empire. In *The Christian Philosopher; or the Connection of Science and Philosophy with Religion*, published in several editions in the 1830s and 1840s, many passages describe Saturn, particularly the rings—how they look from the earth, their size and composition, and the wonderful spectacle they must present when viewed from the surface of the planet itself. Dick calculated that together the planet and its rings could contain a population more than 140 times that of the earth! His conclusion was that "the numerous splendid objects connected with this planet, were not created merely to shed their lustre on naked rocks and barren sands; but that an immense population of intelligent beings is placed in those regions, to enjoy the bounty, and to adore the perfections of their great Creator."[27]

With Saturn's importance in the solar system predicated largely upon its capacity to support a huge population of celestial beings, its inclusion as a symbolic stone on the Salt Lake City temple becomes understandable. Smith's system of graded glories to accommodate all levels of merit is similar to Dick's belief that the inhabitants of the future state belong to different ranks or degrees of intelligence, though Dick thought in terms of pure, rational intelligences, while the Mormons held to the notion of a bodily afterlife, brought about by specific earthly actions—the temple ritual. Smith had also adopted Dick's concept of the plurality of inhabited worlds, worlds which were to be the home of the resurrected. A planet like Saturn could certainly contain the swelling ranks of the Latter-day Saints, which would of course include members of past generations who would be baptized in the temple. What better symbol could be found than Saturn, with its easily identifiable rings, to serve as a reminder of the ultimate destiny of man, which was to become a god himself and rule over his kingdom peopled by his family and ancestors incorporated into the fold through the sacrament of baptism for the dead? On the temple Saturn is thus given a position higher than the other symbolic stones because this is the most exalted state to which one can rise.

Some of the symbolic stones were omitted altogether from the descriptions of the temple. Each elliptical window was to have been framed by a molding resting upon two diminutive columns. In the right angles formed by the meeting of column base and string course are the square and compass (figure 48), the Masonic emblems which Smith had used on the ritual robes in Nauvoo. These may either reflect the traditional Masonic appeal to abide by the Golden Rule and to restrain one's appetites or they may simply refer to the ritual. The proximity of the two tiny columns to these Masonic symbols and the inclusion of columns at all in a medieval system makes the association of these elements with Freemasonry unavoidable. They must represent

48. *Mezzanine window, showing square and compass*

the two brass columns, Jachin and Boaz, which stood sentry at the pronaos of the Temple of Solomon. Together, they symbolize the stability and permanence of the temple.

Two further Masonic symbols are present on the window surrounds of the west facade center tower, the all-seeing eye and two clasped hands (figure 49)—in a Mormon-Masonic grip used during the temple ritual? Though the conventional Mormon explanation offered for the presence of these well-known Masonic emblems is that the eye is a universally understood symbol for the divinity and the hands represent the handshake of fellowship, Mormons as recently as the early twentieth century recognized their Masonic derivation.[28] The Latter-day Saints are extremely sensitive about implications that their ritual and symbolism were in any way influenced by Freemasonry. Such charges have been leveled at them a number of times by members of the Masonic brotherhood and are always vehemently denied, though Mormons do not dispute the historical fact that Smith and other high-ranking Saints were members of the organization at Nauvoo. Freemasons will not accept Mormons into their society, and Masons do not become Mormons. This intransigence on the part of both "secret" societies may help to account for the lack of specific information about the meaning of the temple symbols. All mention of Freemasonry terminated once the Saints had arrived in the valley of the Great Salt Lake. That Young was cognizant of Masonic symbolism, however, there can be no doubt. He was of course one of the men who had belonged to the Nauvoo lodge and had been a Mason in New York state before joining the Mormons.

The temple ornament demonstrates that Young was continuing Joseph Smith's incorporation of selected Masonic devices into the Mormon vocabulary. Though one might wonder why Young wanted to include symbols on the temple which were so patently derived from this source, Masonic symbolism ostensibly refers either to the Bible in general or to the Temple of Solomon, a building which both Mormons and Masons acknowledged as the original sacred structure. Young must have believed that the symbols added a further Old Testament quality to the building and therefore saw no inconsistency in using elements which to him were derived not really from Freemasonry but from a much earlier source.

By transforming the Mormon temple from a formal to a symbolic building, Brigham Young had demonstrated his realization that architecture had great potential for making manifest certain truths about the organization of the cosmos and the laws which govern it. It is not too far-fetched to draw a parallel—in principle at least—between the Salt Lake City temple and the Gothic cathedral in their application of sculptural decoration for didactic purposes and their use of a building as encyclopedic summary of what was known about the universe. Though the immediate reason for the endowing of architecture with

28. A manuscript by D. M. McAllister, A Description of the Great Temple, Salt Lake City, 1904, in the Church Historian's Office, refers to both of these as Masonic symbols.

49. *Detail of the center tower*

content was the association with Freemasonry, the Mormons already had a predilection for symbolism. As millennialists, they regarded the visible world as a metaphor for religious truths and saw in all natural objects and social events the workings of divine purpose. Throughout Mormon literature there is a constant search for evidences of the fulfillment of prophecy in "signs of the times"—natural disasters, governmental upheavals, even scientific inventions—which could be interpreted as preparation for the arrival of the last days.[29] Even the Kirtland temple, not an overtly symbolic building, was felt to have meaning beyond the purely formal and abstract, and this had been even more true of Nauvoo.

But the fate which befell the symbolic stones illustrates the dilemma encountered in trying to impose an already extant system of symbols upon a theology from which they do not naturally arise. One senses that these symbols were invented or appropriated due to a need felt for some kind of symbolic language to visually enrich this new class of architecture, that the desire to give the building meaning prompted the search for forms. There is an air of self-consciousness about these astronomical and Masonic curiosities despite their association with Mormon meanings. With the exception of the sun, moon, and stars, they have no basis in Latter-day Saint theology. Further complications are created by the Masonic meanings of the symbols. For the Freemasons they are part of an ethical construct and are used as aids to remind the members of the rational, moral actions that the members are expected to uphold as part of the fraternity. They can be considered as religious symbols only in the sense that Freemasonry pays homage to an enlightened, deistic God, but they possess nothing of the mystical meaning Brigham Young attached to them. For those Mormons who had been Freemasons there must have been some confusion as to precisely what the stones meant, and for the immigrants coming into the Great Basin from northern Europe they probably had little, if any, significance.

The lack of general comprehension of the meaning of the stones has made it impossible fully to identify all which appear on Angell's drawings. Those which remain unexplained are the stars (some of them with six points) on the battlements, though these may simply be additional "star stones," signifying the telestial kingdom. It is also not known whether there was any significance attached to the number of times each type of stone appears on the building, or why the single points of the five-pointed stars face up on the windows of the towers and down throughout the rest of the building—perhaps another way of distinguishing between the towers and the body of the structure.

The elaborate symbolic stones were rather rapidly abandoned as work progressed on the temple after the death of Brigham Young in 1877. An elevation executed in 1878 by Truman O. Angell, Jr., evidently done in order to study proposals for the mullions in the win-

29. As an example, see the column entitled "Signs of the Times" in the *Millennial Star*, 4, 1 (1840): 73; "Modern inventions and discoveries, for instance, the mariner's compass,-the art of printing,-the discovery of America,-steam navigation and railway travelling, etc., are all so many preparatory steps to open the way for a short work on earth; both as it regards the spread of intelligence, the speed of news, or the expeditious conveyance of those who are to be gathered. . . ." The writer also mentions volcanoes, floods, hail, tornadoes, and the political turmoil in Ireland as signs.

50. *Earth stones as they appear now*

51. South flank, showing earth, sun, moon, and star stones

52. Detail, showing moon stones

53. Beehive motifs on the stairway of the St. George temple

54. *Tabernacle, Manti, Utah*

55. *Detail*

56. Detail of the St. George tabernacle, showing star stones

dows, has had deleted all of the decoration on the battlements as well as the cloud stones on the buttresses at the side of the tower. The columns and compass-square carvings around the elliptical windows were eliminated even earlier, in 1870. By the time the temple was completed, the details of the globes on the earth stones had been changed into the monotonous, scumbled surface seen today (figure 50), so that the stones resemble nothing more than round, decorative disks which could not be identified as symbols of the earth and the gathering without prior knowledge of the designers' original intentions. The sun stones (figure 51) and crescent moons (figure 52) no longer have faces. Symbolic stones were not placed on any other Utah temples, with the exception of St. George, where the newel posts of the staircases are shaped like beehives (figure 53), Mormon-Masonic symbols for industry and the emblem of the state of Deseret. The stones did occasionally appear on other Mormon religious buildings in the nineteenth century, though in abbreviated form and not as part of a complete program like that of Salt Lake City. For example, a tablet on the tower of the Manti tabernacle (figures 54 and 55) displays the eye and handshake, and the entablature of the St. George tabernacle tower (figure 56) is decorated with stars.

As an extension of the visual symbolism of the stones and the towers, it is possible that the proportions of the temple were also to have had meaning. Gowans and Newcomb have made passing reference to the supposedly symbolic proportions of Salt Lake City and Nauvoo, the former asserting that Salt Lake City is "highly symbolic in plan, proportions, forms, and carved emblems."[30] Newcomb, speaking of the Nauvoo temple, states that the dimensions of the building bore some relationship to reputed to restorations of the Temple of Solomon.[31] As far as can be ascertained, however, this does not seem to have played a part in the planning of either building. Enough information is available in I Kings, II Chronicles, and the history of Josephus so that a reasonably convincing facsimile of the Temple of Solomon could have been reconstructed had this been the desire of Brigham Young. By 1854 some archaeological research had been done in Palestine, and the Mormons would not have been altogether ignorant of the appearance of the temple, since they were in possession of several archaeological publications. Yet in no way could the Salt Lake City temple be mistaken for a reconstruction of the Biblical temple in its details, and the proportions of both Salt Lake City and Nauvoo are dissimilar to those of the ancient Hebrew temple.

Smith and Young were more interested in having the Temple of Solomon serve as a functional, not visual, prototype for the Latter-day Saint temple, and since the Saints were distinct from the Jews, they would not have wanted to copy the Biblical building. The Mormons did not purport merely to restore the Old Testament order; they were a creative people who belonged not to ancient Israel, however important

30. Alan Gowans, *Images of American Living* (New York and Philadelphia, 1964), p. 306.
31. Rexford Newcomb, *The Architecture of the Old Northwest Territory* (Chicago, 1950), p. 152.

32. Burton, *The City of the Saints*, p. 253.

were the ties with the Hebrews, but to the latter days, when those things had been revealed to Joseph Smith which the protagonists of the Old Testament had not known. To have fashioned the temple in the image of those belonging to the old dispensation would have been to look backwards toward a defunct era, when in fact Mormon architecture was progressive, anticipating the arrival of a new age and designed to function in it. The Salt Lake City temple, while quoting selectively from the Temple of Solomon in the inclusion of the font and preserving some elements of the architectural tradition the Mormons had already begun to institute at Nauvoo, forcefully declares its differences from other architecture in order to express a world view unique to the Latter-day Saints.

What must now be explained is the style itself—why did the Mormons suddenly abandon the style of the temple they had only recently completed at Nauvoo? William Ward said in 1892 that in building the temple Angell desired to make it look unlike any other building in the world, but it is clearly dependent to some extent upon historical styles. Was the choice of a variant on Gothic purely accidental, a selection of details by Angell from contemporary architectural handbooks illustrating the several medieval alternatives to the Greek Revival, or was it, rather, that Brigham Young determined that Mormon temples would no longer be classical? In the absence of any comments on style by the Mormons, what can be inferred about the meaning of the Gothic on the Salt Lake City temple? Finally, is it possible to find any specific sources, whether in handbooks or actual buildings, which might have influenced the temple?

Nothing in the career of Truman O. Angell prior to 1851, when he assumed the position of church architect, had prepared him for a monumental medievalizing project on the scale of the Salt Lake City temple. From the tenor of his diary it would be difficult to believe that he could have suggested to the church president such a radically new concept. Like William Weeks, his first major building was to be the most important of his life's work. Aside from residential architecture for the president, Angell's commissions included the council hall for the Seventies, described by Burton as "an adobe tenement of the usual barn shape, fifty feet long by thirty internally, used for the various purposes of deliberation, preaching and [social] dancing,"[32] and the old state house at the territorial capital of Fillmore, a rather crude and certainly conventional Greek Revival building, only one wing of which was completed. There is nothing in these structures to indicate that Angell's was the guiding mind in the determination of the temple's style.

The language of the buttresses and battlements points to a collaboration between Angell and a coauthor, probably Brigham Young himself. The evidence provided by the other three Utah temples seems to substantiate this. The insistence upon using the castellated style in the

1880s (when modern buildings like the Richardsonian-style County Building were being erected in Salt Lake City) throws into relief the extreme backwardness of the temple style and designates the crenellations and buttresses as much a part of the Mormon temple style as the towers and the difference in height of the two ends. On all the other temples, the details of the spires were executed in styles which were not consistent with the rest of the building, but the towers and the "cornice" of the building are always Gothic. Manti displays an elegant Second Empire cupola above the battlements, St. George presents a variation of the octagonal tower of Nauvoo, and Logan reverts to a kind of colonially inspired cupola. The architects were apparently allowed some kind of freedom in the decorative details of the temples, that is, those elements which had no doctrinal significance, but were expected to adhere closely to the pattern established by Salt Lake City in other respects.

There are other indications of the strict control Brigham Young exercised over the work of his architects. In a brief resumé of his work as church architect, William H. Folsom, architect of the Manti temple and the design of the tabernacle in Salt Lake City, described his role on the Salt Lake City tabernacle succinctly: "Brigham Young gave me the idea and explained to me what he wanted and I drew up the plans."[33] A franker statement of dependency upon the president could hardly be found. Truman O. Angell, Jr., quarrelled with Young over the Logan plans when the now aged leader insisted upon having his ideas carried out, and Young eventually had his way. Since Young was obviously not interested in having the temples keep pace with contemporary eastern developments, his retention of the castellated style must have had some significance.

Unlike Joseph Smith, Brigham Young had practiced a trade before becoming a full-time servant of the church. As a young man in rural New York he had been apprenticed to a cabinetmaker, painter, and chair manufacturer, and he was known in and around Auburn, New York, for his interior furnishings. Tradition has it that he helped construct, landscape, and decorate many of the farmhouses in the area. The historical person of this most famous Mormon has, however, become so encrusted with legend that no one building can for certain be documented as an authentic work. As a new convert to Mormonism he had helped in the building of the Kirtland temple by supervising the painting of the interior. Though Young could not have been called an architect, he was familiar with the builder's profession and would have been able to form opinions about the appropriateness of styles and motifs.

Isolated though the Mormons were, the architect's office had in its possession (at least by 1877 when Angell temporarily retired) a number of architectural books, some presumably illustrating Gothic details which could have been incorporated into the temple design.

33. Dictation by W. H. Folsom, 1886, manuscript in the Bancroft Library, University of California, Berkeley.

34. "Salt Lake City,"
*Harper's New
Monthly Magazine*
69, 411 (1884): 393.

Angell reported that the possessions included thirteen architectural
books, but, characteristically, omitted any mention of their titles. The
1852 catalogue of the Utah Territorial Library numbered among its
architectural and engineering holdings many of the major contemporary and older publications—Nicholson, Benjamin, Lafever, Shaw,
three of Downing's books, and Fowler's *A Home for All*. The Mormons
thus were not unaware, even in the 1850s, of what had been occurring
in the east, and they had at their disposal a variety of sources with
which to work. However, except for Downing, who illustrated an occa-
sional villa in the castellated style, none of these handbooks give consideration to the use of buttresses and battlements in the way that the
Salt Lake City temple does. In addition, these publications were almost
exclusively pattern books and building manuals, whose purpose was to
provide models for domestic buildings. They do not deal with civic or
religious structures, so they cannot fully account for the creation of the
Mormon temple style.

Visitors to Salt Lake City in the later decades of the nineteenth century, when they were not preoccupied with the issue of polygamy,
would occasionally describe the appearance of the city for those back
east. The most impressive edifice was the temple, whose walls were
slowly rising throughout the seventies and eighties. As an anonymous
correspondent for *Harper's* noted:

> The temple was contrived and sketched out by Brigham Young.
> The style is one unknown to architectural schools, I think, but
> more nearly resembles the Gothic than any other. The structure is
> of cyclopean strength . . . there is no hollowness, or "filling" or
> brickwork—nothing but solid chiseled granite through and
> through, not only the outer walls, but in the partitions, the ceil-
> ings, and the stairways. The window openings are like the embra-
> sures of a fort, and the heavily walled compartments of the base-
> ment suggest the direst dungeons.[34]

The writer quite accurately compared the temple not to ecclesiastical
architecture, but to a fort, whose attributes are strength, solidity, and a
certain air of gloom. Significantly, none of the temples erected in Utah
has any relationship to architecture having religious connotations. The
sources of the Utah style, though not found in the handbooks of
domestic architecture, nevertheless depend upon secular, not sacred,
architecture.

By 1854, the date of the drawings, the Gothic Revival was in full
swing in other parts of America. Ecclesiastical architecture was already departing from the application of Gothic details to what remained essentially a classical mass in favor of the imitations of authentic historical styles, especially early English, in plan, form, and spatial
composition. Church and secular architecture alike were caught up in
the principles of the picturesque, especially as they had been articu-

lated in the writings of Alexander Jackson Downing—the necessity of establishing harmony between building and surroundings, the appropriateness of Gothic as a style of nature, feeling, and sentiment; the delight in asymmetry, texture, and natural color of materials; and the need for "truthfulness" in architecture. Truthfulness, encompassing expression of purpose and revelation of structure, became in Downing's later books the conviction that the work of architecture was capable of exerting a moral influence upon its occupants, a common dictum at mid-century. By the 1850s the Gothic was being assimilated into a panoply of styles—Tuscan, Romanesque, and others—collectively designated as the picturesque.

Despite its combination of round-headed windows, buttresses and crenellations, the Salt Lake City temple is manifestly not a picturesque building. The active skyline of picturesque structures, punctuated by turrets, varied in shape and size, dropping and rising suddenly in extreme contrasts of height, finds no counterpart at Salt Lake City, with its ordered ranks of towers rising in regular, progressively smaller stages to the spires, which continue this rhythmical, restrained upward movement. Asymmetry in the temple is atypical, not the organizing principle, and the only asymmetrical element in an otherwise rigidly regular building, the towers, breaks the balance only slightly and in so doing stresses the uniformity of the remainder of the building. The sides of the temple tend to break down visually into separate, repetitive bay units terminating rather abruptly at the towers.

A further requirement of what Meeks has defined as the esthetic of picturesque eclecticism, besides movement, variety, irregularity, and intricacy, is roughness, with "emphatic stone joints, quarry-faced ashlar, roofs of rough tile or stone. Roughness, if extended to its limit, becomes decay and ruin, the effect of time and the elements, and is, in this sense, 'natural.'"[35] As has been observed, granite was chosen as a substitute for the Salt Lake City temple precisely because it does *not* suggest decay, and little attention was given to the surface texture of the temple. The granite is of a uniformly polished, austere surface with minimal distinction made between the texture of the walls and of the window frame, each block identical to all the others in size, shape, and color—closer to the classical clarity and smoothness of surface of the Greek Revival than to medieval revival buildings. The moldings and string courses add to the studied regularity of the structure rather than contribute variety and interest; they stress the rectilinearity and rigidity of the self-contained mass instead of opening out to nature.

Two other aspects of the picturesque must be assessed with regard to the Salt Lake City temple, the generally felt desire of the mid-nineteenth century for the building to express its structure, to derive its exterior shape from interior plan, and the need for a moral architecture, one which had positive effects upon those who saw and passed through it. The interior-exterior correspondence is nonexistent today

35. Carroll L. V. Meeks, "Picturesque Eclecticism," Art Bulletin 32, 1 (1950): 227.

because of changes in the arrangement of the interior rooms, but even as Angell planned it, there was only the most elementary relationship between interior and exterior elevation. It in no way could be considered an "organic" building, since it lacks almost completely any sense of spaciousness, of the interior working to shape the outside shell. Nor is the expression of structure in any way relevant at Salt Lake City— structure and form are homologous. Nowhere in any Mormon source known to me is there any reference to the potentially beneficial affective power of the Mormon temple. A substantive change of course occurred in the individual who entered into the ritual, but this resulted from the ceremony, not the visual qualities of the architecture.

If, then, the Salt Lake City temple is not a truly representative example of the architecture of the 1850s, how is it to be seen in relation to the rest of American architecture? Little attention has been paid to a phase of the medieval revival which preceded the blossoming of the picturesque but which enjoyed a certain vogue, especially in the second and third decades of the century. This was the castellated style, included in the category of Gothic Revival but with its own distinctive characteristics. Though the Gothic never dominated civic building, there were certain uses to which the castellated style was suited, primarily because of its associative powers. One need think only of John Haviland's Eastern State Penitentiary in Philadelphia, 1821– 1825, A. J. Davis's New York University, 1837 (figure 57), or two rather late examples of the genre, the library at West Point, Isaiah Rogers, 1842, and James Dakin's unique Louisiana State Capitol at Baton Rouge, 1847–50, to realize that the castellated Gothic could summon thoughts of indestructibility and defensibility, governmental authority, or the cloistered life of the medieval scholar. The castellated style as represented by these buildings existed as a transitional mode between the essays in Batty Langley Gothick of the eighteenth century and the mature Gothic Revival and picturesque styles. These medieval revivals before the 1840s depended for source material substantially upon historical works about architecture and the early writings of Pugin, which dealt almost exclusively with Perpendicular Gothic, often secular, buildings. They anticipated the picturesque styles in their broken silhouette and romantic recollection of the past, but did not yet reflect an interest in the structural possibilities of the Gothic. Such buildings were generally biaxially symmetrical, and the battlements and buttresses were still applied to underlying geometric forms reminiscent of the classical tradition.

Clearly the Salt Lake City temple is more closely related to the early endeavors in Gothic than to the styles of the middle of the century. The tracery of the tower windows in the original plans (figure 58), the octagonal corner buttresses on the towers, the narrow, flat buttresses along the sides, the cavetto moldings and the moldings atop the crenellations are all derived from Perpendicular Gothic. Still earlier publica-

57. *Old New York University*

58. Drawing for corner towers

59. Drawings for interior columns

60. *Drawings for windows*

tions, the books of Batty Langley, account for the decorative details under the elliptical windows on the exterior and for most of the interior elements as planned by the elder Angell (figure 59), though the window embrasures (figure 60) seem to have been inspired by early nineteenth-century English books on medieval architecture.

The castellated style was an appropriate choice for a number of reasons. The building was designed to house the secret ritual, and the fortress-like connotations of the castellated style would announce the aim of the Mormons to exclude those who were not properly qualified to enter. The temple sat at the foot of the Wasatch Mountains, with the town spreading out to the sides and below it on the gradually sloping land to the south, the community drawing its inspiration and meaning, as at Nauvoo, from the building which was to dominate its horizon. Salt Lake City was an almost entirely Mormon town, and the battlements and buttresses would have had a similar relationship to the city that a medieval castle had to the agricultural village, asserting its dominance and at the same time its protectiveness. It was certainly successful in communicating to visitors like the *Harper's* correspondent the Mormons' intention to defend their refuge (and it became progressively clearer with the discovery of gold in California and the subsequent opening of the west that the Great Basin was indeed the last refuge for the Saints in America). After their experience in the east, the Mormons understandably anticipated trouble from the gentiles. The fear of invasion was identified with temple-building, for it was the two previously completed temples which had felt the wrath of the gentiles after the Saints had left Kirtland and Nauvoo.

Even before the temple foundations were started, a sandstone and adobe wall was built around the entire temple lot, rising to a height of fifteen feet, which was to be surmounted by a six-foot high picket fence. At the same time, the city council voted unanimously to wall in the entire city "with a good ditch upon the outside of the wall,"[36] a project which says a great deal about the deeply felt apprehension of the early community. This fear was not without basis, for in 1858 the Mormons were in fact "invaded" by the armies of the United States government, sent by President Buchanan to subdue what he had been told was a rebellion (Utah had been annexed as a territory only a year after the Mormons arrived, the consequences of which will figure later in this chapter). No hostilities actually ensued, but when the federal troops entered Salt Lake City for a brief period of occupation, there was no trace of the temple foundations or workshops to be seen—Brigham Young had ordered them buried so as to escape notice and possible destruction by the army.

There were a number of places where Brigham Young could have seen examples of the castellated Gothic if the architect's office did not have any volumes of Pugin or other suitable publications. Before undertaking to move the Saints west, Young had done a great deal of

36. Manuscript History of Brigham Young, 23 August, 1853, Church Historian's Office, Salt Lake City.

travelling throughout the eastern part of the country on missions, and as one of the Twelve Apostles he had been sent to England to assist with the British Mission during the Nauvoo period. While on these journeys Young was of course acting only in the capacity of an upper-echelon priest, not as church president, so there is no convincing reason to believe that he would have used these trips to study the architecture in order to apply what he saw to the particular purposes of the Latter-day Saints. Unfortunately he was as taciturn in his diaries as Angell was, and his journals for this part of his life contribute only the barest skeleton of facts and give no indication of what he may have seen or admired.

There is, however, one category of building to which Young had every reason to be attracted on his trip in 1843. As a long-standing member of the Freemasons, who had very recently had his ties with the fraternity renewed in Nauvoo and had furthermore seen much of the familiar content sanctified by inclusion in the Mormon ritual, it would have been in order for Young to have visited the large and important Masonic lodges in the eastern cities. The three great cities of the east coast, New York, Philadelphia, and Boston, had all witnessed the construction of Masonic temples in the Gothic style in the early years of the nineteenth century. New York's, by Hugh Reinagle, built in 1826, was the least impressive, consisting of a flat, rectangular facade with Gothic details applied to it. Philadelphia's and Boston's were more ambitious, and, significantly, were both in the castellated style (figures 61 and 62).

Why the Freemasons adopted the castellated style has never been explained adequately. Since the Masonic order had been instituted in the seventeenth century, its architectural symbolism was classical. The Masons, for example, appropriated and elaborated upon the Vitruvian values assigned to the orders—Doric representing strength, Ionic, wisdom, and Corinthian, beauty—and found the classical mode eminently suitable for its building purposes. The nineteenth-century change to Gothic (the Philadelphia temple, designed in 1808, was one of the earliest Gothic buildings in America) at a time when the Neoclassical style was itself just gaining popularity may have been prompted by a desire for a less rational, more "mysterious" architecture consonant with the secrecy maintained by the organization. The castellated style conveyed the sense of exclusivity in which the Masons took pride and undoubtedly reflected the new historical awareness of the late eighteenth century, particularly the nascent interest in the medieval past. The Modern Freemasons held that their lodges were derived from the medieval guilds of stonemasons who had worked on the cathedrals and claimed that their ritual was based upon that developed by these practicing artisans as a means of preserving trade secrets. The Gothic style thus expressed the historical continuity of the brotherhood and the legitimacy of their association.

61. Philadelphia Masonic temple

62. Boston Masonic temple

Though different in its disposition of forms, the Philadelphia temple[37] does share with the Salt Lake City temple the battlemented walls, perpendicular tracery, and especially the unusual "fortified" tiered towers with finials at the corners. The Boston Masonic temple, another of Isaiah Rogers's ventures away from the Greek Revival, is also similar to the Salt Lake temple in its handling of the massive stone walls with their deeply recessed windows and in the towers, whose pilaster strips or protobuttresses at the corners define and separate them from the rest of the building in the same fashion as those at Salt Lake City. The towers are divided into three sections by ornamental string courses very much the way in which they appear on Angell's plans.

What makes the connection between Mormon and Masonic architecture even more striking is the inclusion on the Salt Lake City temple of two statue niches on each facade. These are not visible on Angell's drawing, but can be seen on the completed building flanking the center tower, squeezed into the angle formed by the meeting of the tower and body of the building (figure 63). Other drawings by Angell show that each niche was to have been occupied by a standing figure of a nineteenth-century gentleman dressed in a frock coat, one holding a book, the other a cane (figures 64 and 65). They are Joseph and Hyrum Smith, the two Latter-day Saint martyrs. These bronze statues actually remained in the eastern facade niches for a number of years and now stand in the square next to the temple. There are indications that this was, again, an adaptation of a Masonic idea. The proper design of a Masonic temple called for the inclusion on either side of the entranceway of a niche with a statue of St. John the Baptist and St. John the Evangelist, "both of whom were eminent patrons of Freemasonry."[38] (These can be seen in the illustration of the Philadelphia temple.) The Mormon temple seems to have taken up the positioning of the niches and replaced the statues of the Saints with figures more appropriate to Mormonism.

Brigham Young was the head of the Boston mission in 1845, when he learned of Smith's assassination, and had visited Philadelphia in 1843. As a Mason he would have been interested in the temples, especially since a Masonic hall was being built in Nauvoo. When the new president was called upon to act as chief architect for his people, his ideas about the temple's style as well as the symbolic stones must have been affected by the architecture with which the Mormons had the closest kinship, that of the Freemasons.

The castellated style, besides expressing the Mormons' determination to defend their territory and preserve their ritual inviolate, was inseparably tied to the Saints' concept of the destiny of the world and their belief that the Church of Jesus Christ of Latter-day Saints was the instrument which would fulfill the Biblical prophecy of the coming of God's kingdom. When Young declared that his intention was for the

37. The Philadelphia temple was completed in 1811 according to designs by William Strickland. The wooden tower burned in 1819 but was rebuilt by the architect. See Agnes Addison Gilchrist, *William Strickland, Architect and Engineer, 1788–1854* (Philadelphia, 1950), pp. 46–47, 59.
38. James Hardie, *The New Free-Mason's Monitor or, Masonic Guide* (New York, 1818), p. 143.

63. Detail of the east facade, showing statue niche

64. Statue of Joseph Smith

65. Statue of Hyrum Smith

Salt Lake City temple to stand a thousand years, he did not include in the calculations any time which the temple might have to stand *before* the Parousia. This was because the event was, for Mormons as for all millenarians, anticipated in the imminent future. The reign of Christ was to commence almost immediately, perhaps as soon as the temple was finished. Even more than while under Smith's leadership, the Mormons of the early Utah years were obsessed with the subject of the millennium. Smith's promise that Christ would come before the generation at hand had passed away meant that it would have to occur before the turn of the century. In Salt Lake City expectations ran high that the date was to be 1890.

The work of redeeming all mankind by the ritual was to continue in the temple during the millennium, but the function of the temple would be expanded. Joseph Smith seems never to have given much thought to what would happen to the temples in the millennium, but Young, a more methodical and practical man, if more prosaic, wanted to provide for all eventualities. Throughout the history of the Saints, the temples had been referred to as the House of the Lord, a commonly used metaphor in most denominations. But the Mormons were not given to metaphor as such. What Brigham Young meant by the House of the Lord was just that—the residence of the deity. When the temple plans were begun in 1853, Young stated explicitly that Christ might inhabit the building:

> I have determined, by the help of the Lord and this people, to build Him a house. You may ask, "Will he dwell in it?" He may do just as He pleases; it is not my prerogative to dictate to the Lord. But we will build Him a house, that if He pleases to pay us a visit, He may have a place to dwell in, or if He should send any of His servants, we may have suitable accommodations for them.[39]

During the 1850s and 1860s, this idea reappeared, and in more positive terms:

> But what are we here for today? . . . to lay the foundation of a Temple to the Most High God so that when His Son, our Elder Brother shall again appear, he may have a place where he can lay his head, and not only spend a day or night, but find a place of peace, that he may stay till he can say I am satisfied.[40]

> He requires his servant to build Him a house that He can come to , and where He can make known His will. . . . We would like to build a substantial house, suitably arranged and embellished— a permanent house—that shall be renowned for its beauty and excellency to present to the Lord our God.[41]

Clearly, the Salt Lake City temple was to serve as a dwelling-place for Christ when the millennium occurred, and the secular qualities of the

39. *Journal of Discourses*, I (1854), p. 376. Smith had revealed in 1843 that when Christ comes, "we shall see him as he is. We shall see that he is a man like ourselves." *Doctrine and Covenants* 130:1.
40. *Discourses of Brigham Young*, ed. by John Widtsoe (Salt Lake City, 1925), p. 640.
41. *Journal of Discourses*, X (1865), p. 252.

42. One of Brigham
Young's sons, Don
Carlos, was ap-
pointed church ar-
chitect in 1890,
three years after the
elder Angell's death.
What influence (if
any) he had upon
the temple plans is
not known; the
younger Angell con-
tinued to supervise
the construction of
the temple after his
father's death. Don
Carlos built the
temple annex,
1892–1893, which
was rebuilt com-
pletely in 1962. De-
scriptions of the
temple interior are
based on those
found in James
Talmage, *The
House of the Lord*
(Salt Lake City,
1968).

castellated style can now be seen as not only symbolizing the fortress of the Lord, but also the residence of Christ.

The interior of the temple as it was finally built reflected this new function in its more opulent decoration, fittingly palatial, which was planned in the 1880s. By this time Angell's tentative ideas for the ornamentation of the two halls had been abandoned, for conditions necessitated making some changes in the arrangement of rooms. The Salt Lake City temple, though first to be commenced, was the last to be completed, and when the interior was ready to be finished, a variation in the ritual had been introduced. As the temple at St. George neared completion, Young began to think more deeply about the proper performance of the ritual, which was to take place for the first time in Utah in a consecrated temple. He had said repeatedly that there were some ordinances which could not take place in Endowment House, but must wait until a temple was ready. In 1877 he decreed that it was not enough for the dead to receive baptism vicariously, but that they must undergo the sealings and conferring of endowments by proxy. In other words, the entire ritual must be repeated for the deceased. It soon became apparent after the St. George temple was put into operation that the rooms provided in the basement, planned around the baptismal font in a manner similar to the original design of Salt Lake City, were not going to be sufficient for both classes of ritual, and Logan and Manti were designed from the outset to have only one assembly hall, on the second floor, with the remainder of the space to be divided into smaller chambers. As the largest, busiest, and most important temple, Salt Lake City had to be modified during construction in order to function efficiently.

The changes were carried out by Truman O. Angell, Jr., whose plans called for the addition of an annex on the north side of the building for the reception and preliminary preparation of the participants (this was replaced by a larger structure in 1962).[42] The entire basement was to be devoted to the baptismal ceremonies and the font was to be flanked by washing rooms on either side, those on the northwest side for men and on the southwest for women. Some of the ritual which the younger Angell had planned to move upstairs remained in the basement, however, for when the temple was dedicated in 1893, there were two large assembly halls able to seat three hundred people each in the basement. The north is the room where instructions about the ritual are given; it is decorated with scenes of the creation. The south is the Garden Room—the Garden of Eden—painted with scenes of the world before the Fall, where the ritual actually begins.

The remaining rooms to be described are still used in the way originally intended. The first floor (figure 66) is given over to the continuation of the ritual. The participants move up the stairs to the southwest corner, where the large World Room depicts the world after the Fall and before the curse was lifted by the coming of the new dispensation.

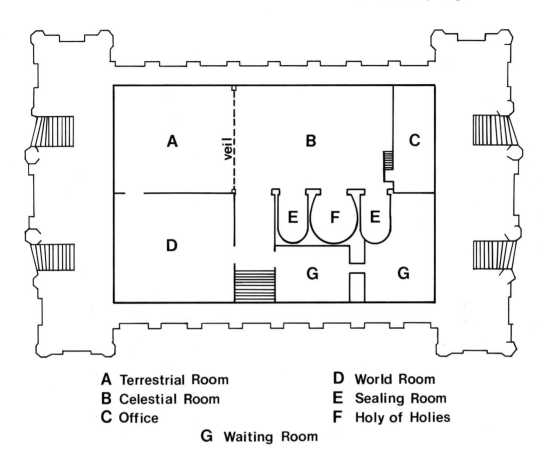

A Terrestrial Room   **D** World Room
B Celestial Room   **E** Sealing Room
C Office   **F** Holy of Holies
              G Waiting Room

66. Conjectural ground plan of the Salt Lake temple

43. Talmage, *The House of the Lord*, p. 162.
44. *Ibid.*, p. 163.

Across the hall to the north is the Terrestrial Room, similar in size and decorated like the World Room with landscape murals. The entire east end of this room is spanned by an arch, which connects it to the most magnificent room in the temple. This is the Celestial Room, which is higher than the rest and must be entered by walking up several steps to the arch. The arch is thirty feet wide and is filled by a curtain, the "Veil" of the temple.

Having passed through the Veil, one is in the Celestial Room, measuring sixty by forty feet. As its name implies, this room is representative of the exalted state and is even more sanctified than the other rooms in the temple. Some idea of its resplendence can be gained from some beautifully rendered drawings in an unidentified hand (figures 67 and 68). This is the most elegantly decorated of all the ritual rooms and is close to its original condition, not having undergone extensive redecoration in the twentieth century, as have several other rooms. It is painted white with gilt trimmings, the walls articulated by moldings, paintings, and fluted Corinthian half-columns placed between mirrors set in alternating segmental and arched frames. The Celestial Room is a far cry from the Nauvoo attic draped with curtains and attests to the overwhelming significance which the performance of the ritual had by this time attained, not to mention the greater prosperity which the Mormons enjoyed.

Could it not also be, however, that the splendor of the temple interior, increasingly elaborate as one approached the Celestial Room, was due to the fact that the arrival of Christ was anticipated, and that he was actually to reside in the temple during the millennium? The Celestial Room looks no more like a religious sanctuary than does an elegant reception hall or state sittingroom of the 1880s, which suggests that its function may have been to serve as the audience hall of Christ, especially since it is through the Veil that the final secrets of the attainment of the celestial kingdom are revealed. At the south end of the Celestial Room are three doors leading to ceremonial chambers. The two side rooms are the sealing room for the living, where marriages are performed, and for the dead, where members of one's family are sealed to the family forever, but the center door leads to the Holy of Holies, a circular chamber with paneled walls and velvet furnishings, which corresponds to the "most sacred precincts of the Tabernacle and Temple in the earlier dispensations."[43] The Holy of Holies is the nucleus of the temple, and with the inclusion of the sacred precinct the transformation of the Mormon temple from the meetinghouse to the Solomonic temple was completed. Exactly what the Holy of Holies is, or how it is used, is kept secret; Talmage says only that it is reserved to the "higher ordinances in the Priesthood relating to the exaltation of both living and dead."[44] It is tempting to speculate that this might be a room reserved for Christ, barred to all "unless he shall say 'Enter ye

67. Drawing of the Celestial Room

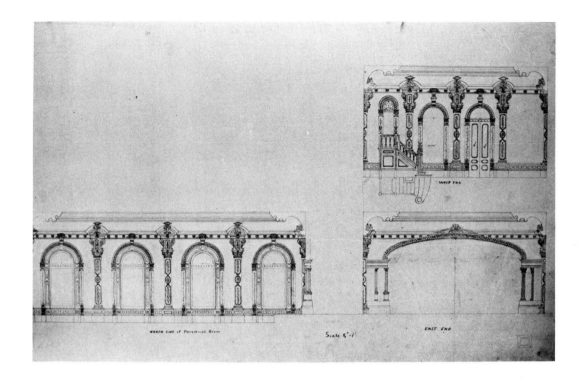

*68. Drawing of the Terrestrial Room and entrance to the Celestial
Room*

into this my house, and there officiate in the ordinances of my Holy Priesthood, as I shall direct.'"[45]

The second story above ground is the mezzanine floor, corresponding to the elliptical windows, where a corridor separates two rows of rooms used for offices and meetings of the priesthoods. The third story is the general assembly room, the only remaining link besides the offices with the interior of the Kirtland temple. The double-ended hall, provided with a gallery, is used primarily for convocations of missionaries about to leave for all parts of the world to expedite the conversion of all peoples to Mormonism, for proselytizing has remained as important for the Saints in the twentieth century as the gathering was when the establishment of the kingdom of God seemed to be imminent.

The kingdom of God, with Christ as its legitimate ruler, retained the Mormons' political allegiance even while Utah was being incorporated into the boundaries of the United States. Deliberately having chosen to go beyond the territorial limits of the United States to set up his community, Brigham Young learned early in 1848 that the Great Basin Region had been annexed by Washington, and the Saints were faced with their perennial problem of compromise and conflict with the government of the world. Their response was to petition Congress immediately for the incorporation of Utah as a territory, hoping by this means to avoid the onus of a territorial governor appointed from Washington and to keep through elections the theocratic control which already existed. In asking for official territorial status the Mormons were not being hypocritical, for both Smith and Young believed that the government of God would eventually absorb, not overthrow, the American government and would in fact be the instrument that preserved the democratic ideals of the Constitution, which Mormons felt had been perverted. Eventual statehood could also be considered as a step towards this end.

The Mormons did not wait for a territorial government to be set up for them; even as the petition for admission was being drawn up, the Council of Fifty created its own civil government (precisely the reason why the Mormons had moved to Utah) and had actually instituted its own independent state. The state of Deseret—Deseret was the Mormons' word for honeybee—was established "in order to realize as many of the ideals of the political kingdom of God as possible before affiliation with the United States."[46] A constitution was drawn up by a convention whose members all belonged to the Council of Fifty, and the state assembly as well as the governor (Brigham Young) and other officers were hand-picked by this skeleton governing mechanism of the kingdom of God. The ambition of Deseret far outdistanced its potential at this time, for the state claimed as its domain all of Utah and Nevada, portions of Idaho, and a strip of land cutting across New

45. Brigham Young, in *Journal of Discourses*, X (1865), p. 252.
46. Klaus J. Hansen, *Quest for Empire*, p. 127. Much of the material contained in this book is summarized in Hansen's "The Metamorphosis of the Kingdom of God: Toward a Reinterpretation of Mormon History," *Dialogue*, 1, 3 (1966): 63–83.

47. Gustive O. Larson, "Federal Government Efforts to 'Americanize' Utah Before Admission to Statehood," *Brigham Young University Studies* 10, 2 (1970): 22.

Mexico and Arizona to San Bernardino, California, which would provide this new state easy access to the sea and make it more like a self-sufficient nation than a state (figure 69). The Council also resuscitated the Nauvoo Legion at the same time. During 1849 and 1850 Deseret was totally independent, untouched by the federal government.

In 1849, before any decision had been made in Washington about what Utah was to become, the Mormons asked to be admitted to the Union as a state, not a territory, hoping to use the doctrine of states rights to maintain independence for the area. However, insufficient population and a dislike of rule by the Mormon hierarchy led Congress to organize Utah as a territory. Deseret was dissolved in 1851 after the denial of statehood, but this was not the end of the Saints' dream of an independent nation-state. Salt Lake City was host to numerous federally appointed administrators and judges, but the real authority was still exercised by the church. The Council of Fifty remained in operation throughout the fifties and sixties, working to insure economic independence for the kingdom of God.

The outbreak of the Civil War quickened the hopes of the Saints that the millennium approached, for this was read as the ultimate "sign of the times," which was leading to the final conflagration and the collapse of the governments of the world. In 1861 the church revived the legislature of Deseret, which remained operative until it became clear that the end was not yet at hand. Hansen has convincingly demonstrated that Deseret was in fact the nucleus of the kingdom of God and the seat of Zion, that the Mormons were actually implementing the principles of the government of the Lord by carrying on the secret activities of the Council in expectation of assuming world rule as a millennial legislature under the aegis of Christ himself, for it is apparent from speeches given by the Mormon leaders that Christ was to assume control of the political kingdom. In 1863 Young explicitly stated that the Saints were bypassing the territorial government which had been established, and that the true governing body of Utah existed underground:

> We meet here in our second Annual Legislature, and I do not care whether you pass any laws this session or not, but I do not wish you to lose one inch of ground you have gained in your organization, but hold fast to it, for this is the Kingdom of God. . . . We are called the State Legislature, but when the time comes, we shall be called the Kingdom of God.[47]

A shift in the Latter-day Saints' concept of Zion had been occurring since the arrival in Salt Lake City. When the Mormons referred to Zion in the 1830s, they meant Independence, Missouri. While at Nauvoo and still thinking of themselves as part of the United States, America

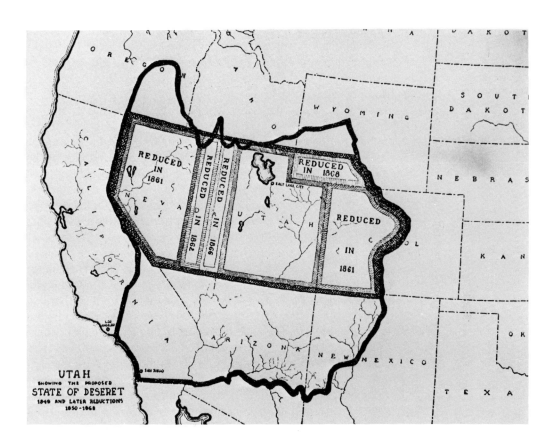

69. Map of the State of Deseret, from Leland Creer, Utah and the
Nation

48. Milton R.
Hunter, "The Mor-
mon Corridor," in
*Utah, A Centennial
History*, ed. by
Wain Sutton (New
York, 1949), I, p.
477, reprinted from
*Pacific Historical
Review* 8 (1939):
179–200.
49. *Ibid.*, p. 484.

in general began to be regarded as the land of Zion, though the holy city itself would be in Missouri. After the establishment of Salt Lake City, the Mormons continued to pay lip-service to the idea of Zion at Independence and held out the hope of eventually returning there to erect the temple planned by Joseph Smith, but such a move was not contemplated in the near future. Increasingly, Zion was identified with Utah, not the midwest. Attention was turned to building up the kingdom in other ways than by the creation of the Deseret legislature.

Passive anticipation of the millennium had never been a part of the Mormon ethic—to the contrary, active participation had always been stressed. In this respect, the Mormons should be regarded as "premillennialists," those who believe that changes must be effected by man before the millennium can commence. Millenarians like the Millerites watched and waited, expecting divine intervention at an arbitrarily ordained moment. The Saints certainly gave thought to the external evidence of the approach of the last days as witnessed in natural catastrophes, political turmoil, and other signs, but a large part of the rationale behind the building up of the kingdom was the conviction that the great event would not transpire unless things were set right. In the sparsely populated west, the aims of the kingdom of God began to look more and more like those of a thriving and vigorous earthly utopia. Young was anxious to introduce industries into the valley which would promote the economic independence of the area. The church encouraged the development of paper and textile mills, foundries, and other enterprises which could enable the Mormons to live without importing from the east.

Brigham Young's dedication to his vision of the kingdom prompted him to begin its establishment even while the Salt Lake settlement was still struggling for survival. In 1849 he started to implement the claims of Deseret by populating what has been called the "Mormon Corridor,"[48] a line of settlements along the route from Salt Lake City to the Pacific Ocean at San Diego. "By spring of 1855 twenty communities running in a direct line from Salt Lake to Cedar City [in southern Utah], a distance of 265 miles, were connected by a good wagon road, and the road had been extended on to the Pacific coast."[49] During the Utah war Young recalled the San Bernardino Valley settlement, but with the passing of immediate danger the towns were gradually advanced, though California was abandoned when it became a state in the Union.

An interesting thing about the Mormon Corridor is that a concomitant program of temple-building was instituted, or at least projected, along with the settlements. The three later Utah temples are all built along this route, St. George at the last outpost of Mormon colonization in the south, Manti approximately in the center of the state, and Logan on an extension of the corridor to the north, on the way to Idaho. Definite planning for these three temples was begun in the 1870s, but there are indications that they were proposed some time earlier. In the case of Manti there are references in 1852 to a temple block which had been set aside and was going to be walled in 1854. Brigham Young prophesied the building of the Logan temple in 1863 and hoped that "in the process of time the shores of the Pacific may be overlooked from the Temple of the Lord."[50] These temples, in other words, were to be part of the building up of the state of Deseret and kingdom of God.

Church President John Taylor advanced in 1881 what has become the conventional Mormon explanation as to why the temples were built in other parts of Utah besides Salt Lake City. Referring to the St. George temple, he said:

> It was found that our temple in Salt Lake City would take such a long time to build, it was thought best to erect one down here. Why? Because there was a people living here who were more worthy than any others. . . . God inspired President Young to build a temple here because of the fidelity and self-abnegation of the people; and, furthermore, that there might be an asylum here for those living further south to be administered to the holy ordinances of God.[51]

This explanation, that the temple was a kind of reward for the people of southern Utah and that it was needed to accommodate the growing population, overlooks a significant fact. The Mormon colonization of the valleys of Utah was an operation directed by fiat, not a haphazard process of expansion. In the case of St. George, the entire town was established by volunteers and conscripted families from the Salt Lake City area who were exhorted by the church leaders to leave their property and move south. In 1871, when the St. George temple foundations were dug, there were only eleven hundred inhabitants, not even enough to construct the temple. Most of its construction was carried out by men from other parts of Utah who had been sent to St. George specifically to build the temple. One has only to look at a photograph of the Manti temple in process of construction (figure 70) to perceive that a structure of its scale and magnificence was not at all warranted by the town itself. Manti as late as 1888 was a rude frontier village with nowhere near the number of people which the temple could accommodate. It gained much of its population as well as a newspaper and a library while the temple was being constructed. In all cases, the temple *preceded* the influx of people into the area, and even today these towns remain relatively small in size.

These efforts at Logan, Manti, and St. George were being expended at the same time that work on the Salt Lake City temple was progressing by inches. Since this labor was available, there must have been another reason why it was not directed towards finishing the first and

50. Journal History, 7 August, 1847, Church Historian's Office, Salt Lake City.

51. *Journal of Discourses*, XXIII (1881), p. 14.

70. Manti temple in process of construction

most important temple before three completely new buildings were
started. Reading further in Taylor's discourses, the answer is found:

52. *Ibid.*

> There was another thing. In establishing the kingdom of God, it
> was necessary that there should be a strong place somewhere be-
> tween the land south and the land north. It was necessary that
> there should be a foothold here all through these valleys of the
> mountains between Salt Lake City and north of Salt Lake clear
> away, as you have heard President Young say, on the backbone of
> the American continent . . . furthermore, President Young ex-
> pected that these railroads that are now coming would come
> along. . . . And if there had not been some pretty strong places . . .
> we would never have been able to carry out the will of God. . . .[52]

In this passage Taylor assigns to the temples a function which has
nothing to do with their ritualistic purposes. He states that the temples
themselves were to be outposts of the kingdom of God, manifestations
of the Council of Fifty and the government of Christ on earth. His
explanation that the settlements with their temples were to be "strong
places," if considered in conjunction with political and economic
events in Utah, makes evident why there was a sudden enthusiasm for
temple building in the 1870s and 1880s along the arteries of the old
state of Deseret.

With the completion of the first transcontinental railroad at Promontory Point, Utah, in 1869, Utah was irrevocably involved with the
United States. The railroad opened up the Great Basin to gentile im-
migration and potential exploitation, a trend vigorously opposed by
Young and the older members of the church. The Council of Fifty
continued in operation throughout the seventies, but younger, more
liberal Mormons began to agitate for an end to isolationism, and, as an
inevitable accompaniment, the abandonment of the kingdom of God.
Gentile political organizations added external pressure to the division
within the Mormon ranks. In 1870 the Liberal Party was formed to
combat the political dominance of the church hierarchy; the Mormons
were still able to frustrate their attempt to send one of their candidates
to Washington. At the same time a concerted effort by enemies within
the United States tried to end the theocracy by attacking the social
order of the kingdom—polygamy—though Mormon claims that persecution by the gentiles was due solely to their unconventional marriage
patterns is not totally accurate. The diatribes against the Saints were
due also to the prevailing, and correct, belief that government in Utah
was not democratic.

The evidence strongly suggests that the St. George, Logan, and
Manti temples were built in response to threats to the kingdom of God.
They were started in the early 1870s, immediately after the coming of
the railroad, and were completed surprisingly quickly in the 1880s, at
the time of greatest challenge to the authority of the kingdom, proba-

bly to strengthen the boundaries of the kingdom and assert to its own people and to outsiders the continuing vigor of the millennial utopia. The castellated style, deliberately retardataire, was a visual extension of the central jurisdiction of Salt Lake City, the capital of the kingdom, and may be understood as the official governmental style of the kingdom of Christ on earth. The smaller size and less elaborate program of decoration of the later Utah temples express their subsidiary relationship to Salt Lake City, the center stake of Zion. They were, in a sense, provincial capitals, outposts of the holy city at strategic points in the territory. Laying claim to the land in the name of the Lord, their distinctly secular qualities suggested the merging of church and state in the millennium.

Chapter 6

Temples of the Kingdom of God: St. George, Logan, and Manti

St. George, Logan, and Manti, though similar, exhibit qualitative differences in the way each architect adapted the architecture of his time to the requirements of the kingdom of God. The St. George temple was begun while Truman Angell was still functioning as chief architect, and he drew up the plans. The builders of the other two temples had come up through the ranks of the church architect's office in Salt Lake City, so construction of the temples remained strictly with the Mormon community. The Logan temple was the domain of Angell's son, who had gained his knowledge of architecture by working as head mason on the Salt Lake City temple and who seems to have had no experience as an independent architect. William Harrison Folsom, in charge of Manti, was also a product of the Salt Lake City workshop, though he had worked outside the church for a time.

The concerted effort at colonizing the St. George area started in 1861. Brigham young visited the Rio Virgin Valley and foresaw there a city "with spires, towers, and steeples . . ."[1] which he hoped would accompany the growth of the cotton industry he proposed to promote in this mild climate, the so-called "Dixie" region of Utah. The Dixie mission struggled along through the 1860s and in the spring of 1871 was informed that a temple was to be built there. A letter followed from Brigham Young with dimensions and specifications for the building, which was to be almost identical to the interior of the Salt Lake City temple, but smaller. That fall Young journeyed to St. George and selected a site in a marshy area, claiming the spot had previously been dedicated by the Nephites. The section and facade elevation (figures 71 and 72) were drawn up in Salt Lake City and s' nt by the architect to St. George. After this he had little to do with the construction, as he was too busy with his other work. Matters were left in the hands of the head mason, E. L. Parry.

If St. George (figures 73 through 79) looks primitive by comparison with the other temples, at least part of the reason is that it was hurriedly constructed, a rush job pushed through by the authorities in Salt Lake City. At the dedication of the site in November 1871, Young expressed his wish that it be far enough completed in twelve months to

1. Kirk M. Curtis, "History of the St. George Temple" (M.S. thesis, Brigham Young University, 1964), p. 23.

71. Preliminary design for the St. George temple

72. *Cross-section of the St. George temple*

73. St. George temple

74. *Side elevation of the St. George temple*

75. *Facade, St. George temple, showing inset arched panels in central tower*

76. Old photograph of the St. George temple

77. *Detail of the St. George temple tower*

78. St. George temple from the north, showing annex

79. Flank of the St. George temple

administer ordinances, and other leaders speculated that the entire structure could be completed in two years. The president was an old man by this time, and the desire to see a temple sanctified and functioning must have been especially urgent for him. When it became clear that this would not be enough time, Saints all over Utah were exhorted to contribute their labor. Parry reported that painters, carpenters, and plasterers came from as far away as the Cache Valley in northern Utah to work on the temple.

The St. George temple exterior established its relationship to its prototype without mimicking it. The side elevation (figure 74), though starker, is almost the same as the Salt Lake City temple, with the double-storied mezzanine arrangement of eight bays and the half-length basement windows. There is also a vestigial pediment on either end, two doors on the eastern facade, castellations, and buttresses. At St. George, however, there is a definite sense of direction, a designation of one of the facades as an entrance—here and in other aspects of the building the influence of Kirtland and Nauvoo (both of which the architect knew very well) dominates.

The drawing for the facade shows a very broad, low, and rather disjunct arrangement of forms. The style, described by the head mason as "modern Gothick,"[2] manifests a certain self-conscious medievalizing of forms. The tower suggests a Gothic spire which has somehow been swallowed up by its base, for there are no transitional elements to modify the abrupt juxtaposing of shapes. Angell was not at home in the Gothic style, for the proportions of the facade still seem classical. The inset arched panels in the central tower (figure 75) betray the consistency of the time lag between Angell's architecture and contemporary developments. This motif and the triple-arched window it contains were popular in the 1850s during the revival of the various round-arched styles, but 1871 is a very late date for these abstracted, undecorated shapes to appear. The arched windows are certainly a deliberate reference to the "Palladian" windows at Kirtland, though they now seem to be a romanesque variant of the originally Georgian motif.

As can be seen in a photograph taken sometime before 1885 (figure 76), when an annex was constructed at the north side of the temple, the central tower is different from that shown on the drawing. Whether the tower was actually built as Angell planned it and then was altered is not known. The spire of the drawing has been replaced by an octagonal cupola with engaged columns at the corners, reminiscent of Nauvoo, but the uncomfortable truncation of the first design remains. In 1883 it was replaced according to specifications provided by Folsom, then at work on the Manti temple. This is a somewhat more satisfactory solution (figure 77), perhaps the best that could be found, given the existing conditions. The battlements of the tower base were removed and in their place a more delicate open balustrade introduced, which was repeated on a smaller scale around the top of the lantern.

2. E. L. Parry to D. H. Wells, 7 June, 1876, letter, Church Historian's Office, Salt Lake City.

3. A. W. Musser,
"From the Presi-
dent's Party,"
Juvenile Instructor,
11, 10 (1886): 107.

The cupola was elevated upon an octagonal base of slender proportions (making the reference to Nauvoo even stronger), richly ornamented with dentilling, moldings, and quatrefoils. The details and proportions of the present tower are in themselves more pleasing, but the tower is far too narrow for the base upon which it rests, and contradicts the fortified mass topped by battlements.

The buildings as a whole is less massive than Salt Lake City, in part simply because it is on a smaller scale—the walls are three instead of eight feet thick; the tower 135 feet high—and because the heavy stone construction is visually negated to a significant extent by the plastered and whitewashed surface. Volcanic rock was driven into the marshy ground to anchor the foundations, and the portion above ground was constructed of red sandstone quarried from about two miles outside the city. The stone, chosen because of its resistance to decay, was then whitewashed so as to make it "truly beautiful."[3] The integration of the temple into the city has decreased what must have been its effect as a sentinel along the road to the south and west. The grounds of the building are now carefully landscaped and the view of the temple is obstructed by the annex and visitors center (figure 78), where information about Mormonism is dispensed to tourists who stop to look at the temple. The side elevations, with their incessant, repetitious bay units, are less active than Salt Lake City. There are no decorative string courses, no symbolic stones, and even the window surrounds are unadorned. Yet St. George does possess its own severe beauty, its abstract shapes and contrasts of wall with the voids of window openings, seen in the strong sunlight of southern Utah, creating brilliant oppositions of light and shadow unlike any of the other temples (figure 79).

The interior as built came closest of all the temples to the original plans for Salt Lake City. The basement contained the font and was entered by four doors, two on either side. Before the first floor was remodeled in 1938 and converted into endowment rooms, both stories had simple halls supported on cast-iron bundled columns similar to those drawn by Angell for the Salt Lake City temple. The floor plans were nearly identical with those of Kirtland and Nauvoo. From the time of its dedication in 1877, however, its overwhelmingly important use was for the ritual, especially baptism for the dead. The first baptisms performed were for the signers of the Declaration of Independence and the presidents of the United States.

The church architect's office was in a state of flux while plans for the temples at Logan and Manti were being formulated. Joseph A. Young had been appointed architect and superintendent for the Manti temple in June 1875, but he died at Manti in August while making preliminary surveys and plans. At about the same time, Brigham Young accepted Angell's resignation as church architect, designating Truman O. Angell, Jr., to serve in his father's stead. After a quarrel with the president over salary (Angell's son, a generation younger than the pioneers, disliked voluntary labor, and Young was furious that he wanted some kind of compensation beyond the knowledge that he was doing the Lord's work), Angell was relieved of his position. Folsom took the job, along with Truman Angell, Sr., who agreed to return to work to act in an advisory capacity. In 1877 Folsom was put in charge of the Manti temple.

Folsom was almost as old as Truman Angell and had been with Joseph Smith in Nauvoo. Born in 1815 at Portsmouth, New Hampshire, he had had the typical New England-New York experience of most of the early converts. Moving with his parents to Buffalo, he became a Mormon in either 1841 or 1843 and went to Nauvoo to work on the temple. Following the demise of Nauvoo he worked as a contractor and builder in California and Nevada between 1849 and 1860. For the six years after 1860 he was church architect in Salt Lake City during the temporary retirement of Angell because of poor health. Along with Henry Grow, an engineer, he designed the tabernacle inside the temple block. After a short period of absence from church service, Folsom began the construction of Manti and was associated with it until its completion.

The Manti site was as difficult to deal with as St. George, but Young said that it was sanctified because Moroni had dedicated it. Before construction could begin, the rattlesnake-infested top of a hill had to be leveled. Blasting and excavating were started in the spring of 1877, and by June 1880 the font room was up to full height. The capstone was ready to be set in place three years later, but then work tapered off. The church stakes in the vicinity of the three outlying Utah temples had been organized into temple districts and were charged with financing construction and securing labor, all of which was voluntary. The Manti temple was constantly owing money for supplies, and the matter of finances was the problem most on Folsom's mind during the years of construction. Not until late in 1887 was the masonry work completed, and the temple was dedicated on 21 May 1888.

Brigham Young had died in 1877. Even so, his was the directing force behind Logan and Manti, as it had been for the others. There is only one plan for the Manti temple, and no drawings which have yet come to light. The extant plan is not even one which Folsom used while at work on the building, for it was sent to President John Taylor after Young's death to indicate how the basement, with its ritual rooms, was to be built, "as directed and supervised by Brigham Young."[4] Folsom stated in the accompanying letter that he was "told by President Young that he intended to have the Manti and Logan temple alike, that is the inside, or plans of convenience of Performing the labours therein."[5]

Contemporaneously with Manti, and with fewer attendant difficulties, the Logan temple was rising several hundred miles to the north. Situated in a valley yet close to the mountains, Logan, Utah, was a

4. Signed, undated drawing by Folsom in the Church Historian's Office.
5. W. H. Folsom to John Taylor, 24 May, 1878, letter in the Church Historian's Office.

town similar in character to both St. George and Manti. Logan was particularly secure in the Cache Valley for it was surrounded on all sides by rugged terrain and had to be approached from the other towns of Utah Territory through a mountain pass north of Ogden. The choice of Logan rather than Ogden for the site of the temple is especially telling. It was Ogden, not Logan, which was the economic center of northern Utah, for it lay in the Great Basin, easily accessible from Salt Lake City and strategically placed just south of the continental railroad line. But Ogden was a boom town, raucous and swarming with outsiders, too busy and full of transients to serve as a city of the kingdom of God. Young and his counselors selected the site for the temple in May 1877, only one month after the same ceremony had taken place at Manti. Foundations were dug at once, and the laying of the cornerstone took place in September 1877, after Young's death. Present at the occasion was the assistant church architect, Truman Angell, Jr., whom Young had reinstated as architect in charge of Salt Lake City and placed as overseer of Logan. Construction proceeded more rapidly here, and the Logan temple was dedicated in May 1884.

The lack of preliminary drawings makes it impossible to hypothesize about the process of designing the temple. The similarity in proportions and dimensions between Logan and Manti, the octagonal auxiliary towers, and the return to the double-ended form suggest that Angell and Folsom may have been working in concert. Both architects were present at the dedication of the Manti site, which points to at least some degree of communication. Besides the interior arrangements of the temples, it is not known what other specific requirements —size, for example—were imposed upon the architects by Young. How much freedom they had after the church president's death is also uncertain, but John Taylor was anxious to follow the plans as developed by his predecessor, and he exercised control over at least the functional aspects of the buildings.

The plans for both temples called for the inclusion of a separate small building to serve as an annex for heating apparatus, offices, reception rooms, and a room for preparatory ceremonies before the ritual began in the temple proper. Here, and at the annexes added to Salt Lake City and St. George, a passageway led directly from the annex into the basement, facilitating the progress of the ritual and making it easier to check the credentials of the entrants. Built for purely practical reasons, the annex extricated all mundane functions from the sacred building. Since the annex was planned in advance at Logan and Manti, there was no real need for two doors on either facade, especially since now the temples were planned without the lower assembly hall with its double-ended pulpits and two aisles. However, Manti's eastern facade (figure 84) has two doors, as do both identical facades at Logan. Their retention may have been a symbolic reference to the sexual segregation practiced throughout the temple rites.

The younger Angell's temple shows the affinity for his father's work at St. George primarily in the center towers (figures 80 and 81). Returning to the double-ended arrangement of Salt Lake City, with symbolically higher eastern towers, each end facade at Logan displays a variant of the Kirtland Palladian window set into recessed panels, though here each story introduces a subtle distinction in shape and type of mullion. A single narrow window, similar in shape and size to the windows of the side elevation and the two lower stories of the side towers, reflects by its decreased width the dropping away of the rest of the building behind the third level of the tower, which ascends to support a wooden cupola. The base of the cupola repeats the blind-arcade motif of the tower of St. George. The cupola itself, a strange conglomerate of colonial forms, Doric pilasters, and battlements, perches atop the cornice like the brim of a hat. Its squared-off shapes continue those of the tower proper and the battlements link it to the lower portions. By the addition of a third level to the tower, the entire center section becomes more slender and vertical, a tendency which echoes late nineteenth-century developments in the rest of the country.

Despite its attenuation in the center towers it is, in its details, a far more authentic English castellated structure than either of the two earlier temples; its angle buttresses on the center towers and corners of the rectangular "nave," its octagonal side towers, and the cavetto moldings acting as string courses to separate the various levels are all part of this vocabulary. The local sandstone used, an irregularly colored light brown, creates a slightly weathered look with a pleasing variation in natural colors and textures. The flanks of the temple (figure 81) pay homage to the original two-story elevation of the Kirtland temple and represent, in purely architectural terms, a more pleasing solution to the problem of the articulation of the sides than Salt Lake City. The number of bays has been reduced from eight to seven, mezzanine windows are left out, and the length of the remaining windows has been increased to absorb most of the area of the wall, which consolidates the elevation into distinct, uncluttered stories. The result, however, is that the true nature of the interior is disguised, for it is not possible to determine where the offices are located and where the ritual takes place. What is from the outside ostensibly the first floor is actually a staggered series of progressively higher small ritual rooms occupying two floors, with the third given over to the Celestial Room (called, in this temple, the "C" Room). The undifferentiated exterior is, then, the final concealment of the interior functions of the temple.

Without question, William Harrison Folsom was the most sophisticated architect working for the Mormons. Even more than Logan, the Manti temple demonstrates the provincial architect's adeptness and originality in working with a unique form and in an outmoded style, both of which he reconciled with contemporary ideas to produce an imposing and truly monumental building. Although dealing with a

80. Logan temple

81. Logan temple

difficult site, Folsom nevertheless used it advantageously to increase the dramatic appearance of both site and temple. The temple was to be situated approximately halfway up the side of the hill north of town on an artificially leveled plateau, with the hill abruptly resuming its natural curves immediately behind the building. The architect had somehow to accommodate the terrain to the double-ended format and prevent the building from being visually consumed by the hill. A further problem was one of orientation. The promontory upon which the temple would sit overlooked the Sevier Valley to the west, and the eastern facade would abut the hill behind it. The facade which one would expect to be dominant—that overlooking the valley and town— was supposed by virtue of direction to be the less important end of the temple.

Folsom dealt with the problem of terrain by blasting out four levels of terraces (visible in figure 70) and enclosing them with walls around three sides of the temple. The foundations of the temple were sixty- three feet above the rest of the town, and the terracing increased the impression of height. It was intended that shrubs and flowers be planted on the terraces, and fountains were contemplated to further beautify the surroundings. The terracing was removed in 1907 and the hill transformed into a gentle slope (figure 82), so that the full effect of what should have been a grandiose ceremonial approach has been lost. On the eastern end, square towers allow the temple to fit against the hill at right angles without the awkwardness which would have occur- red had octagonal towers been employed. Thus the transition from man-made terracing to natural contours is effected with greater ease, as the building is at once anchored against the hill. In so doing, Folsom also addressed himself to the problem of the greater height of the east- ern end, for the nonidentical facades distract attention from the fact that the eastern end is actually higher. Instead of greatly increasing the size of the towers themselves, the symbolic difference is expressed primarily by the addition of a spire. The building *appears* to be facing west towards the valley, not towards the mountain; the slightly greater height of the eastern end merely picks up the downward slope of the hill and continues it to the western end, where it is assumed by the terraces.

Further accommodation was made to the site by giving the temple a complete three-story elevation. The basement windows are no longer a truncated suggestion of the subterranean level, for they have risen above ground and are almost as tall as the other stories. This elevates the two "main" stories high enough so that they are not dwarfed by their setting and produces the effect that the building rests on a base. The two upper stories are not of a uniform size, so the effect of the sides is of a rather subtle gradation of height from ground level to cor- nice, with each higher story increasing in size. Folsom was careful to indicate that the basement is not truly equivalent to the higher stories

82. *Manti temple from the south*

by not extending it along the entire length of the building. Instead, at the eastern end, an arch on the lower level of the side towers stops the movement of the basement windows and leads into the hill, raising the assembly floor almost to the level of the hill behind it.

The eastern and western facades are quite different from one another. The western (figure 83) is four stories high (five, if the cupola is included) with proportions of pronounced verticality emphasized by the pointed mullions set within the long, narrow windows. The two "main" stories are distinguished from the others by the slightly greater length of their windows and the height of their segments of the towers. Windows and empty niches on the octagonal towers, decorative devices which possibly allude to the statues niches on the Salt Lake City temple, diminish the massiveness of the walls by puncturing them with many recessed openings. The eastern facade (figure 84) is a closer quotation from the earlier temples—two doors with individual staircases, small basement windows, and the generally more compact and horizontal proportions. Since the doors on this facade do lead directly onto the level of the assembly hall, they may have been intended as entranceways, though there is no record of their having been used as such. (Note also the use of false paneling above the door to increase the vertical movement, figure 85.) Here, as at Logan, it is interesting to observe how insignificant the relationship between exterior and interior has become, for in the windows of the facade's central portion are visible two sections of the flooring cutting across them on the inside.

Detailing on the Manti temple is handled with greater sureness and precision than at Logan. Folsom never allowed the castellations to dominate the decorative scheme of the building and worked to make them but one feature of several amalgamated styles which comprise the total structure. The crisp moldings just below the battlements emphasize the rectangularity of the structure underneath, especially at the corners (figure 86), where the buttresses are set back far enough to frame the corner angles. Beneath the battlements a broad entablature with dentilling and a protruding cornice further minimize the Gothic effect of the buttresses, which have become merely decoration applied over an underlying classical system of ornament. Similarly on the facades the towers terminate in a classical entablature carried by modified Tuscan pilasters. Pilasters of sorts appear on the tower lanterns but belong to no order.

The cupolas themselves (figure 87) are an adaptation of the bracketed cupolas found on the Italianate villa, elongated to lend the structure a more "public" character, with the repetition of the round-arched window in the lantern and the roof adding further to the loftiness of the whole. The graceful mansard roofs, thus elevated above the battlements, mitigate the potential severity of the building by their elegant curves and decorative window frames. The towers with their ac-

83. West facade of the Manti temple

84. East facade of the Manti temple

85. Detail

86. Detail

87. Detail

6. Carroll L. V. Meeks, "Picturesque Eclecticism," *Art Bulletin*, 32, 1 (1950): 233, notes that architecture of the sixties and seventies exhibited a "notable preference for verticality achieved on the exterior by suppressing horizontal lines, or by crowding thin windows between buttresslike elements; or by continuing wall motifs above the cornice and crowning the steep roofs with a multitude of incidents."

tive rooflines direct attention to the upper portions of the building, the more so because of the relative uniformity of the three-story elevation below, whose light, but rich, tan walls of local oolite limestone contrast with the slate blue of the mansard roofs.

Finally what distinguishes Manti from the other Utah temples is the extent to which this temple, isolated in the middle of the Sevier Valley in central Utah, shares the characteristics of the Second Empire style of the late 1860s and 1870s. Manti, more than any of the other temples, is a contemporary building, despite its castellations. The motifs which it employs—mansard roofs, a central "corps de logis" to which the side towers are subordinated, the extravagantly embroidered cupolas—are all part of the vocabulary of the French Second Empire in America. Furthermore, its verticality, accentuated by the extension of the windows of the main stories to almost the entire length of the floors and the broken contours of the battlement level, belong to the architectural aesthetic of the late nineteenth century.[6] These qualities are actually quite subdued in comparison to many of the buildings of this time, due to the need to express strength and permanence, and, as will be seen, to certain important considerations of the relationship between the building and its site.

Folsom, more than either of the Angells, truly understood the aims of architecture for the kingdom of God, for there is no element of the Manti temple which can in any way be associated with an ecclesiastical building. The towers no longer refer to the spire of a church and the proportions are not those of a conventional religious structure. The Masonic influences contributing to the appearance of the Salt Lake City temple have been totally absorbed and diffused. Even the style suggests the uniqueness of the temple, for the Second Empire was used elsewhere in the country exclusively for civic or domestic buildings, not for churches. Its use here emphasizes the residential-governmental nature of the building. A thoroughly eclectic edifice, the temple borrows and recombines historical motifs in a resultant nonrevival building which can only be called Mormon in style.

In the absence of any commentary by Folsom or the Angells about their aesthetic aims, it is instructive to turn to the church leaders for insights about what was desired of the temples and what they saw when looking at them. The sources of remarks about the building are the discourses of the president and his counselors, the speeches given at temple dedications, and a few brief reports in the church periodicals. Noticeably missing in all is any description of style or decorative elements. The two parts of the buildings which do catch the writer or speaker's eye are the towers and battlements, though these do not bespeak any specifically historical associations. For the anonymous author of an article in the May 1884 issue of the *Logan Journal*, the temple in that town was a magnificent building:

Precisely what style of architecture the temple belongs to would perhaps be difficult to state. It might be described as of the castellated style, its towers and battlements justifying such classification. Its aspect is lofty, clear cut, and severely chaste, and combines grace and majesty in splendid harmony.

George A. Smith, speaking to a congregation in Salt Lake City about that temple predicted that "the building will be a majestic one, and will creditably compare with any large building in the world."[7] Another writer found it "colossal, mysterious and unique."[8] These are certainly only the most general descriptions, stressing size and grandeur.

However, further extracts begin to hint at an important way in which the temples should be seen in the landscape of the Great Basin. Regarding Manti, one observer said:

> The whole site, with the terraces and the steps from one to another, crowned with the Temple at the back, under the immediate shelter of the mountain, when finished according to design, and the reach of the valley west, north, and south, will constitute one of the finest landscapes anywhere to be seen.[9]

The *Deseret News* reported:

> The building will present a grand and imposing appearance, and as it will be on an eminence, will be in view from the most northern part of the valley, a distance of thirty-five miles.[10]
> It will command a magnificent and extended view, and will itself be seen from a great distance.[11]

At the groundbreaking of the Logan temple site, John Taylor, who had recently succeeded Brigham Young to the presidency, spoke about the newly completed temple at St. George:

> In my visit south to attend conference, I felt to rejoice exceedingly in seeing the temple completed at St. George. It is a most beautiful building, pure and white as the driven snow, both outside and in. It is elegant in design, and there is a manifest propriety and adaptability in all its arrangements. . . .
> Approaching from the north with the black basaltic lava mountains frowning on the background, and the grim red sandstone nearer to its base, relieved indeed by the beautiful city of St. George, with its shrubberies, it stands as a chaste memorial, a sacred elysium, a haven of repose on this beautiful oasis of the desert. . . .[12]

Taylor's response to the sight of the St. George temple contains several significant ideas. Like Manti, St. George was supposed to be seen from afar, visible as one approached from far up or down the valley (figure 89), an object outstanding in its natural surroundings by virtue

7. *Journal of Discourses*, XVI (1874), p. 280.

8. Hannah T. King, "Architecture," *The Contributor* (October, 1882): 39.

9. *Journal History*, 13 December, 1877, Church Historian's Office.

10. *Ibid.*, 6 June, 1878.

11. *Ibid.*, 5 October, 1877.

12. Joseph Hall and Samuel Roskelly, "The Temple of the Lord, Erected at Logan, Cache County, Utah. The History of its Construction from the Foundation to the Dome—A Description of the Sacred Edifice, 1877–1884," typescript, n.d., p. 6, Church Historian's Office.

13. *Ibid.*, p. 23.
14. *Journal History*, 19 November, 1877.
15. Leo Marx, *The Machine in the Garden* (New York, 1964).
16. *Ibid.*, p. 112.

of its purity of form and nonnatural color. All of the Utah temples, especially those outside Salt Lake City, are designed to be seen against the striking background of the mountain ranges. Manti stands atop the highest promontory in the vicinity of the town, and the plateau where the Logan temple was built rises ninety feet above the center of the town (figure 80). Furthermore the whitewashing of the St. George temple constituted a conscious denial of the identification of the building with its surroundings—the temple is distinct from the environment and is not intended to be merged with it. This was not the case simply because the sandstone was a rather coarse medium. It was a consistent way of treating the temples, for Logan and Manti, built of finely textured and colored stone, were also given artificial colors. In the 1880s it was reported that the dark walls of Logan "have been painted a light and pleasing tint, consisting of white softened with a little red paint."[13] Whether Manti was actually painted is not recorded, but the plans called for its being tinted a light yellow-buff color.[14]

This desire to have the temples stand out visibly from a far distance is characteristic of the Mormon response to nature and the relationship of man to the land, the opposing sides of which are closely linked in Taylor's reaction to the sight of St. George. Arriving from Salt Lake City, what Taylor saw first was the desert, formidable and desolate, relieved only by the sight of St. George and its temple marking the locus of a fruitful, flowering oasis. Here we have the conventional antithesis in the Mormon view of nature, the opposition of the garden and the desert, a concept derived from some of the very earliest of American beliefs about the uninhabited territory which lay to the west.

Leo Marx, in *The Machine in the Garden*,[15] traces the evolution of this dichotomy in American thinking back to the Elizabethans, whose reports of the new continent reflected one of two opposing points of view. The most common was to regard America as a great garden of unbelievable fertility and beauty, ripe for cultivation by a civilized race in search of a Virgilian haven remote from the oppressions of the degenerate urban society of Europe. The myth of the garden as it developed in eighteenth-century America inspired visions of an agrarian empire populated by the idealized figure of the farmer, an image which continued to possess the minds of Americans even after it had ceased to describe accurately the realities of an increasingly commercialized and industrialized America. Crevecoeur, Jefferson, and their contemporaries envisioned an ideal society made possible by the richness of the land, existing in a middle state between primitiveness and sophistication, a country of landholding, virtuous, and democratic yeomen. For them, ideal nature was a cultivated nature, a "fusion of work and spontaneous process."[16]

The other viewpoint focused upon the desert—if there was Virginia, there was also New England, described in literature as a howling wilderness, barren and hellish. As Marx proposes:

This violent image expresses a need to mobilize energy, postpone immediate pleasure, and rehearse the perils and purposes of the community. Life in a garden is relaxed, quiet, and sweet . . . but survival in a howling desert demands action, the unceasing manipulation and mastery of the forces of nature. Colonies established in the desert require aggressive, intellectual, controlled, and well-disciplined people. It is hardly surprising that the New England Puritans favored the hideous wilderness image of the American Landscape.[17]

17. *Ibid.*, p. 43.
18. Perry Miller, *Nature's Nation* (Cambridge, 1967), p. 109.
19. *Ibid.*, p. 110.
20. William Mulder and A. Russell Mortensen, eds., *Among the Mormons* (New York, 1958), pp. 69–70.

A modified image of the desert gained particular strength at the end of the eighteenth century, at the time of the Second Great Awakening, and had a profound influence upon the rhetoric of revivalism. The need for salvation, attempts to create a Christian, egalitarian utopia, and millennial expectations were all given a greater urgency of fulfillment as it became clear that America would inevitably press further than the settled areas of the eastern seaboard into the wilderness of the "terrifying West."[18] The churches "had to find a means for combating what everybody feared would be a plunge into barbarism, on the other side of the Appalachians, in a vast area stretching away from Europe. In the next decade [after the Revolutionary War] the cry for saving the West swelled to a chorus of incitation infinitely more impassioned than had been the call for resistance to England."[19] The frontier was a stimulus, then, not only to establish an agrarian, Jeffersonian empire, but, for some, to embark upon a holy mission to wrest territory away from the devil.

The Latter-day Saints' fascination with the religious analogue of the myth of the garden, the American continent as the Garden of Eden, has already been shown to have had a decisive part in the shaping of Mormon doctrine. Accompanying this idea, however, one also finds the opposing strain of the wilderness, apparent in Mormon thought beginning with Joseph Smith. Smith's description of the Land of Zion written during a visit to Missouri contains all the imagery of both mythologies. The first sight of the Great Plains fills him with momentary chagrin:

> Our reflections were many, coming as we had from a highly culti-
> vated state of society in the east, and standing now upon the
> confines or western limits of the United States, and looking into
> the vast wilderness of those that sat in darkness; how natural it
> was to observe the degradation, leanness of intellect, ferocity, and
> jealousy of a people that were nearly a century behind times, and
> to feel for those who roamed about without the benefit of civiliza-
> tion, refinement, or religion; yea, and exclaim in the language of
> the prophets; "When will the wilderness blossom as the rose?
> When will Zion be built up in her glory, and where will Thy tem-
> ple stand, unto which all nations shall come in the last days?"[20]

21. *Ibid.*, p. 70.
22. *Ibid.*
23. *Ibid.*, pp. 70–71.

Immediately after this preface, Smith turns to enumerating the bountiful beauty of the landscape, a landscape unlike anything he had seen in the east:

> As far as the eye can reach the beautiful rolling prairies lie spread out like a sea of meadow; and are decorated with a growth of flowers so gorgeous and grand as to exceed description. . . . The shrubbery is beautiful, and consists in part of plums, grapes, crab apple, and persimmons. . . . Horses, cattle and hogs, though of an inferior breed, are tolerably plentiful and seem nearly to raise themselves by grazing upon the bottoms in winter. . . . Turkeys, geese, swans, ducks, yea a variety of the feathered tribe, are among the rich abundance that grace the delightful regions of this goodly land—the heritage of the children of God.[21]

Nineteenth-century, religiously inspired man that he was, Smith was not content to contemplate the beauties of nature in its pristine state, for action was required:

> . . . the land of Zion bids fair—when the curse is taken from the land—to become one of the most blessed places on the globe . . . were the virtues of the inhabitants only equal to the blessings of the Lord which He permits to crown the industry of those inhabitants, there would be a measure of the good things of life for the benefit of the Saints, full, pressed down, and running over, even an hundredfold.[22]

Here are the standard elements of religious thinking about nature in the early nineteenth century—the wealth of the land, the barbarity of those living there in the natural state without the benefits of civilization, and most important for Mormon thought, the call for action which this state inspires, the need to redeem nature. For Smith, nature is not a moral force, but something which must be transformed through industry, purified, and reclaimed by the hand of God working through his chosen people. The disadvantages of the land of Zion, "as in all new countries, are self-evident—lack of mills and schools; together with the natural privations and inconveniences which the hand of industry, the refinement of society, and the polish of science, overcome."[23] Only when the soil is tilled, towns are founded, and righteousness prevails, only then will the land revert to its state of innocence of the first days. The building up of Zion and, significantly, the erecting of a temple to consecrate the land, must be accomplished first. The city of Zion which Smith planned at Independence was to effect precisely this kind of transformation.

That the Mormons in the Great Basin continued to regard nature as an adversary is not surprising, not only because of their isolation from contemporary thought glorifying nature, but because of the realities of the situation in and around Salt Lake City. The mid-nineteenth century romanticizing of wilderness landscape began in the cities and remained essentially a nostalgic, urban response to the already accomplished destruction of natural beauty. The Saints, however, as the first settlers in the intermountain west, retained, to some extent, the typical pioneer reaction of hostility towards one's surroundings. Nature in the west was not hospitable, it *did* need to be overcome in order to provide a living for the Saints, and it was never celebrated by the Mormons in the nineteenth century.

The image of the wilderness, especially that of the desert, became even more potent in the latter part of the century. For one thing, the rugged terrain of the Utah valleys seemed to corroborate the testimony of Isaiah 2:2 that Zion would be established in the mountains, for ". . . it shall come to pass in the last days, That the mountain of the Lord's house Shall be established in the top of the mountains, And shall be exalted above the hills; and all nations shall flow unto it." The long trek across the plains after the expulsion from Nauvoo and the subsequent settlement in what appeared to be a wasteland had its equivalent for the Mormons in the wandering of the nation of Israel after the exodus prior to the arrival in the Promised Land. The desert also provided a place where the Saints could be safe from the gentiles while building up the kingdom. Thus at the dedication of the St. George temple site George A. Smith thanked the Lord for the desert land, "that we are permitted to shelter ourselves from the enemies of Thy cause."[24] George Q. Cannon proposed expanding settlements into Arizona because:

> . . . While in the circumstances in which we are at present placed, good countries are not for us. The worst places in the land we can probably get, and we must develop them. If we were to find good country, how long would it be before the wicked would want it, and seek to strip us of our possessions? If there be deserts in Arizona, thank God for the deserts.[25]

In fact the image of the desert was exaggerated by the Saints. Much of the Utah territory was actually quite promising, for there were ample sources of irrigation which could transform the area around Salt Lake City into a productive agricultural region, and the valleys to the north and south were lush and beautiful. But the official Mormon view was that the land was sterile and forbidding.

> We came to these mountains because we had no other place to go. We had to leave our homes and possessions on the fertile lands of Illinois to make our dwelling places in these desert wilds, on barren, sterile plains amid lofty, rugged mountains.[26]

By regarding the area as desert, the Saints consequently were able to magnify any improvements made on the terrain and to see all progress as evidence of God's favoring their efforts to make Utah a garden. "We

24. *Journal History*, 9 November, 1881.
25. *Journal of Discourses*, XVI (1874), p. 143.
26. *Discourses of Brigham Young*, pp. 737–738.

27. *Ibid.*, p. 739–
740.
28. *Ibid.*, p. 453.

prayed over the land, and dedicated it and the water, air and every-thing pertaining to them unto the Lord, and the smiles of heaven rested on the land and it became productive, and today yields us the best of grain, fruit and vegetables,"[27] Young declared.

The Mormons never, until the turn of the century, abandoned their concept of the perfect society which had been set forth in Smith's plans for Independence. Brigham Young's Great Basin kingdom was actually more closely related to Zion at Independence than to the holy city of Nauvoo, for it was a rural society based on agriculture, with manufacturing (and cities) encouraged only to the extent necessary to promote self-sufficiency. Throughout the 1850s and 1860s the efforts of the Mormon leaders were directed towards transforming the desert into the garden. The Saints were exhorted to labor for this aim, for the Lord "has done his share of the work; he has surrounded us with the elements containing wheat, meat, flax, wool ... everything with which to build up, beautify and glorify Zion of the last days, and it is our business to mould these elements to our wants and necessities. . . . In this way will the Lord bring again Zion upon earth, and in no other."[28]

One of the most interesting aspects of Mormonism in the Great Basin is the extent to which the society fashioned by Brigham Young was able to resist the pressures of the outside world—even after the railroads had opened up the territory—especially the impulse to move towards a capitalist economy. Young and the Mormon hierarchy realized in the 1850s that the valleys of Utah were neither extensive nor fertile enough to compete with the agricultural regions of the midwest once the latter's products were rendered cheap and accessible by the railroads, nor was Mormon manufacturing efficient enough to combat the flood of inexpensive imported manufactured goods which was expected. The real potential of the area lay in exploiting the rich mineral resources of the Wasatch Mountains, a direction encouraged by the liberal Mormons desiring an end to isolationism.

Nevertheless, Brigham Young refused to contenance such propos-als. His response was to resuscitate communitarian economic organi-zation in the form of the United Order of Enoch and initiate the cooperative movement whereby Mormons patronized those industries and mercantile establishments operated by Mormons in order to keep capital in the hands of the church and prevent commercialization of the region. As Leonard Arrington explains in his extensive study of economics in the Great Basin:

> This spread of cooperation, it must be emphasized, was not a "natural" development. Cooperation was deliberately promoted by the church as a solution to its problems, both spiritual and mate-rial. Cooperation, it was believed, would increase production . . . and make possible a superior organization of resources. It was also

calculated to heighten the spirit of unity and "temporal oneness" of the Saints and promote the kind of brotherhood without which the Kingdom could not be built.[29]

When the mines, owned mostly by non-Mormons, were opened up in the 1870s, Mormons were encouraged by their bishops to seek employment there, but not purely for reasons of profit. Mormon mine labor would prevent the large-scale importation of outside help and would keep money in Utah. With the cash earned for their work, the Saints were told to buy land, stock, and agricultural machinery—elements, Young believed, of a stable, permanent, and moral society which could be bound by tight theocratic control. In the 1870s the Mormon economy was "relatively self-sufficient and much more egalitarian than contemporary American society, the church was still more or less in control of the economy, and the devotion of the citizenry to church and Kingdom appears to have been as great as during the 1850s and 1860s."[30] The Mormons had come close to achieving a kind of Jeffersonian state of existence, "free of the tyranny of the market."[31]

What must not be forgotten, however, is the religious nature of the Mormon landscape, the equating of this garden of America with the Garden of Eden. In 1853 Young had stated the goals of the Saints thus:

> They calculate to operate, and continue to operate, with all the ability, skill, ingenuity, and power that God pleases to bestow upon them, until they accomplish every laudable object on earth, and have made it like the Garden of Eden; until they decorate it with vineyards, and orchards, and every kind of shrubbery, and beautiful, sweet scented flower, and every kind of delicious fruit; until they have made everything that is necessary for ornament, to decorate the persons of the saints, and the palaces, and Temples of Zion.[32]

Like Joseph Smith in 1831, Young envisioned the garden with the inclusion of habitations and temples, an important part of the landscape and necessary in the process of the redemption of the earth. At the laying of the cornerstones of the Logan temple, D. H. Wells offered a prayer in which the presence of the temples was explicitly tied to the process of salvation of the world as well as its inhabitants:

> . . . let our hearts be raised in praise and thanksgiving . . . that the work commenced by the Prophet Joseph still continues and will continue henceforth and forever . . . and the erection of temples to continue, and the purposes of the Almighty be developed and consummated, until, finally the whole program shall be accomplished, the earth reclaimed and its inhabitants sanctified and redeemed.[33]

The Mormon ideal of nature was of civilized, cultivated, pastoral nature, nature wrested from its wilderness (ungodly) state by the hand

29. Leonard Arrington, *Great Basin Kingdom* (Cambridge, 1958), p. 315.
30. *Ibid.*, p. 353.
31. Marx, *The Machine in the Garden*, p. 127.
32. *Journal History*, 10 April, 1853.
33. Hall and Roskelly, "The Temple of the Lord . . ." p. 15.

34. *Ibid.*, p. 2.

of God working through his chosen people, nature consecrated by the epic of sacred history which had previously been acted out upon it by the protagonists of the Book of Mormon. (The Saints were even more convinced of the truth of Smith's gospel by the numerous artifacts of ancient civilization, such as the pictographs which they found carved upon the canyon walls of Utah.) Wilderness nature for the Mormons was not nature in its original state. During the era when God's grace had still been upon the earth, Utah had looked like what the Mormons set about reestablishing—a valley covered with fine towns and cities, the soil tilled by hard-working, righteous people, the original Americans. The land had returned to wilderness because of iniquity, though it could again become the garden. Thus the cosmic drama of mankind was not manifested for the Saints in the natural wonders of Utah, which certainly possesses one of the most varied and spectacular natural landscapes anywhere on the continent. The typical nineteenth-century romantic association was not made; the Saints never experienced the sublime in nature, nor were there any expressions of delight in wild scenery. Mormon society never produced any landscape paintings exciting wonder and awe, even though this was the heyday of Church, Bierstadt, and the panorama. The Mormon view of the relationship between man and his surroundings was essentially pragmatic, not poetic—it is only in architecture that the Mormons made a significant and original contribution to the visual arts of America.

It is no wonder, then, that the Utah temples with their rigidly geometric shapes, their battlements and towers, and their deliberate exclusion of the space around them from the sculptural form of the building, assert the dominance of man over his surroundings, not his identification with, or immersion in, them. Logan, St. George, and Manti (figures 80, 88, and 89) are only three of hundreds of temples which were to cover the land of Zion during the millennium. They were to be seen against their background of mountains and foreground of "sacred elysium," and the view from their towers would encompass the "glorious valley, filled with cities and villages, occupied by tens of thousands of Latter-day Saints. . . ."[34] This was the architecture of a true religious utopia, architecture whose function was to preside over the process of the purification of the earth and the transformation of its inhabitants into citizens of the kingdom of God. Authoritarian, and expressive of a theocratic government, it is nevertheless architecture whose aim was to bring about an ultimately democratic—and peculiarly American—society. The people who built the Utah temples optimistically anticipated the perpetual improvement of mankind throughout eternity, abolition of inequalities, just rewards, and sharing of wealth. The Utah temples, in their isolation, represent the redirection of architecture towards the true purpose of America, the building of a modern-day paradise.

88. St. George

89. Manti

Chapter 7

Epilogue

The dedication of the Salt Lake City temple on 6 April 1893 marked the sixty-third anniversary of the church and the fortieth year after the laying of the temple's cornerstone. Saints converged upon Salt Lake City by the thousands to participate in the ceremonies, which continued for two weeks so as to accommodate all who had arrived for the occasion. The church president, Wilford Woodruff, who had succeeded John Taylor in 1887, delivered the dedicatory prayer—a lengthy invocation of blessings upon the building, the Saints, and the operations of the church. But the closing passages struck a new and conciliatory note, one quite different from the aggressive and militant pronouncements of the Saints of earlier years. Woodruff prayed for increased understanding of the Saints by their fellow citizens and promised that the Saints would reciprocate:

> Show unto them that we are their friends, that we love liberty, that we will join with them in upholding the rights of the people, the Constitution and laws of our country; and give unto us and our children increased disposition to always be loyal, and to do everything in our power to maintain constitutional rights and the freedom of all within the confines of this great republic.[1]

The completion and dedication of the Salt Lake City temple, though a triumphant culmination of years of labor, can only have been an anticlimax, for many of the beliefs for which the temple stood had already been rendered obsolete. Taylor's pledge of loyalty in the dedicatory prayer was in effect an acknowledgment of defeat in certain crucial areas. The very success of the kingdom of God had made it intolerable to the federal government, and as the territories around Utah were admitted to the union, it was inevitable that a decisive conflict would ensue. Public opinion had become increasingly vituperative over the issue of polygamy, especially as inroads were made into the territory by other churches. The federal government saw that polygamy could be used to divest the Mormon hierarchy of its political and judicial power.

In 1887 the Edmunds-Tucker act outlawed polygamy and disen-

1. James Talmage, *The House of the Lord* (Salt Lake City, 1968), p. 141.

2. Klaus J. Hansen, "The Metamorphosis of the Kingdom of God: Toward a Reinterpretation of Mormon History," *Dialogue* 1, 3 (1966): 64.

franchised any who continued to practice it. Since all the important and powerful Mormons were polygamists, they were placed in a difficult situation, for the act not only deprived them of control of Utah, but effectively outlawed the kingdom of God and its social order. The initial response for many polygamists was to go underground, but some kind of accommodation to the realities of the situation was needed, and the church gave in. In 1890 Woodruff issued a manifesto disassociating the church from this practice which had once been of vital importance. The abandonment of polygamy opened the way for admission to statehood, and Utah joined the Union in 1896. Capitulation on this point was no doubt responsible for the successful assimilation of the Mormons into American life and for their ability to maintain considerable political control over Utah in the twentieth century.

There has been considerably less interest in the history of the Mormons of the postpolygamy era. No study has been made of precisely how the Saints were able to recoup their rather devastating political, economic, and psychological losses suffered with the triumph of the United States government. Klaus Hansen has suggested that the twenty years after 1890 "marked Mormon history . . . conclusively and permanently because they witnessed the decline and virtual disappearance of the idea of the political kingdom of God."[2] The crucial shifts in emphasis seem to have involved the abandonment of some of the beliefs which were visually embodied in the Utah temples.

By 1893 even the millennial hopes of the Saints were beginning to fade. When the expected event did not occur, disillusionment set in, and the anticipation of an imminent Second Coming ceased to be a truly vital aspect of Latter-day Saint religion. Today's Mormons still refer to the present time as the last days, but the signs of the times are no longer read with such excitement. More important, perhaps, is that the building of a temple is no longer regarded as an instrumental step in hastening the millennium. Temple-building is now determined by practical concerns—a new temple is constructed when and where the number of Latter-day Saints requires.

Accompanying the decline of millennialism was the transformation of the idea of the kingdom of God from one possessing political and temporal implications to one which more nearly approaches the metaphorical meaning of other religions. Without doubt the increasing numbers of non-Mormons in Utah contributed to this, but there were other reasons within the church itself. The younger generation of Saints in the Great Basin, who had not experienced the earlier difficulties and persecutions, were probably responsible in part for the adoption of more conventional patriotic attitudes towards the American government. With this shifting of loyalties the kingdom of God was no longer tenable as a political concept, and the twentieth-century temples have consistently avoided any motifs suggesting governmental aspirations like those so militantly proclaimed by the Salt Lake City temple.

The intense concern of the nineteenth-century Saints for the acquisition of territory upon which physically to create the ideal society has diminished in the twentieth century with the increased mobility of the American population. Though Utah and the western states remain the center of Mormonism, recent times have witnessed a reversal of the westward migratory pattern of the Saints.[3] There are now a great many Latter-day Saints who reside east of the Mississippi, so that rather than stressing the need for physical concentration to establish the temporal kingdom, the church has directed its attention towards creating a sense of community within the larger American context by encouraging, and even demanding, participation in church affairs. Since the dispersed membership of the Mormons would render a temporal kingdom an impossibility, the gathering is now brought to the rest of the world through the construction of temples outside Utah, and even beyond the territorial limits of the United States. America, though still the land of promise, has lost its exclusivity.

For today's Latter-day Saints, "building up the kingdom" has come to signify professional success, and indeed, the most recent temples have about them the slickness of modern commercial buildings, especially banks and insurance companies, a similarity not inappropriate, for it is in such institutions that a great deal of the church's power resides. The architectural critic of the *New York Times* found that the use of the Gothic pointed arch throughout the new Washington, D.C., temple (in an about-face of the reason for Gothic at the Salt Lake City temple), "to give the place more of the feeling of a church, one of the architects explains . . . suggests nothing so much as those corporate headquarters that endeavor to work their trademark into every possible aspect of their design."[4] With its expensive materials and futuristic forms, it is, he says, "as if the architects had tried to design Buck Rogers's church."

Mormon utopianism has been replaced in the twentieth century by an almost obsessive interest in the afterlife and a greater spiritualizing of theology (though there have been no great revelations handed down to significantly change theology or practice since the nineteenth century). As a legacy of polygamy, the family is the all-important unit in Mormon life, and it is the duty of every Mormon to marry and have many children in order to provide earthly bodies for inhabitants of the spirit world. The importance of baptism for the dead has turned the Saints toward genealogical research with a passion. Church members are encouraged to seek out and copy records of births and deaths of distant ancestors. These names and dates are processed in the temples at an astounding rate. In the Salt Lake City temple, where baptisms and endowments for the dead have been computerized, over thirty

3. Thomas F. O'Dea, *The Mormons* (Chicago, 1957), p. 118.

4. Paul Goldberger, "New Mormon Temple: $15-Million Conversation Piece," *New York Times*, 12 November, 1974.

thousand a month receive these rites. Marriages for time and eternity and the sealing of family members to one another are the other important ceremonies performed in the temples, which are regarded as way-stations in the eternal journey where instructions are delivered without which the journey cannot proceed.

Vestiges of nineteenth-century symbolism mark present-day buildings, though not the temples. The new high-rise church office building a block away from Temple Square displays two gigantic maps of the world on its facade, symbolism reminiscent of the earth stones on the nearby temple. The visitors' center on Temple Square contains grotesque exhibits like the statue of Christ placed in a circular room which is painted with swirling clouds and heavenly bodies (figure 90). However, it is doubtful that many Latter-day Saints comprehend the original meaning of such symbols, and few who participate in the temple ceremonies are aware that the celestial kingdom for which they prepare once included all temporal matters within its scope.

90. *Display in the Visitors Center, Salt Lake City*

Notes

Chapter 1

The basic scriptures of the Latter-day Saints, besides the Bible, are the writings of Joseph Smith—the Book of Mormon, *Doctrine and Covenants*, and the *Pearl of Great Price*. The *Doctrine and Covenants* first appeared in 1833 under the title *Book of Commandments* and was enlarged and given its present title in 1835. Successive editions have added revelations so that the current edition now contains one hundred thirty-four entries from the lifetime of Smith, an account of his assassination, and one revelation by his successor as prophet and president, Brigham Young. The *Pearl of Great Price* contains several revelations, Smith's translations of two "lost" books of the Bible from Egyptian hieroglyphic manuscripts, and a brief history of his early life, especially the finding of the golden plates and the appearance of heavenly emissaries. Smith's journals have been edited and published in six volumes under the title *History of the Church of Jesus Christ of Latter-day Saints* (Salt Lake City, 1908). The official compendium of doctrine is James E. Talmage, *Articles of Faith*.

The Mormons have been a topic of interest ever since rumors began to circulate around Palmyra, N.Y. that young Joseph Smith had found a treasure on his father's farm. Later nineteenth-century stories of polygamy and other outrages to Victorian sensibilities excited the curiosity of Americans and Europeans alike. There are scores of contemporary histories, travel books, exposes, etc., of varying degrees of accuracy. Many of these make very interesting reading, but for more impartial histories of the Saints one must turn to the twentieth century. Two general books of worth are Thomas F. O'Dea, *The Mormons* (Chicago, 1957) and Ray B. West, *Kingdom of the Saints* (New York, 1957). The best biography of Smith is Fawn M. Brodie, *No Man Knows My History: The Life of Joseph Smith the Mormon Prophet*, originally published in 1945.

Whitney Cross, *The Burned-Over District: The Social and Intellectual History of Enthusiastic Religion in Western New York* (Ithaca, 1950), is the most complete study of the phenomenon of the Second Great Awakening in western New York. For the utopian and religious sects of the nineteenth century, see Mark Holloway, *Heavens on Earth: Utopian Communities in America, 1680–1880* (New York, 1951). Interest in American millennial thought has been increasing, as is evidenced by the number of works cited in David E. Smith, "A Bibliography of Millennialism," *American Quarterly*, 17, 3

(1965): 535–549. Of general interest are H. Richard Niebuhr, *The Kingdom of God in America* (Hamden, Conn., 1956), and Ira V. Brown, "Watchers for the Second Coming: The Millennarian Tradition in America," *Mississippi Valley Historical Review*. 39, 3 (1952): 441–458. Ernest Lee Tuveson, *Redeemer Nation: The Idea of America's Millennial Role* (Chicago and London, 1968), traces the development of millennialism in America, primarily through literary analysis, and distinguishes between two kinds of millennial currents: millennarianism, which expected the physical return of Christ, as did the Mormons, and millennialism, which believed that the last age would occur as a natural process of history without a cataclysm. How this belief in heaven on earth was transformed into the advocacy of reform to accomplish the same results is explained in Timothy Smith, *Revivalism and Social Reform in Mid-Nineteenth-Century America* (New York, 1957). The theme of America as a new Eden is taken up in Charles L. Sanford, *The Quest for Paradise: Europe and the American Moral Imagination* (Urbana, Ill., 1961) and Leo Marx, *The Machine in the Garden* (New York, 1964).

The general fascination with Indian mounds and the theories which were current about a lost civilization are discussed in Robert Silverberg, *Mound Builders of America* (New York, 1968) and Curtis Dahl, "Mound Builders, Mormons, and William Cullen Bryant," *New England Quarterly* 34, 2 (1961). Also see Brodie, *No Man Knows My History*, Chapter III. One of the most popular theories held that the Indians were the descendants of the Hebrews and that western New York had been the scene of a great massacre of a peaceful, refined race by warlike tribes. Smith's Book of Mormon grew out of this tradition and thus was credible to a wide audience.

Chapter 2

Though there has been no study of the architecture of the Latter-day Saints, there are several published works which deal with the temples. Two handbooks by Mormon authors, James E. Talmage, *The House of the Lord* (Salt Lake City, 1968) and N. B. Lundwall, *Temples of the Most High* (Salt Lake City, 1941) include historical sketches of the nineteenth and twentieth-century temples, giving dates of the ground-breaking, dedication, etc. Talmage also describes the dimensions and interior arrangement of each building. Wallace A. Raynor, *The Everlasting Spires* (Salt Lake City, 1965) is a history of the construction of the Salt Lake City temple. Mention should also be made of the church publication *Ensign* (formerly the *Improvement Era*), which has published a number of very brief descriptive and historical articles about the individual temples.

Almost all of the primary source material pertaining to the temples is located in the Latter-day Saints Church Historian's Office in Salt Lake City. There are several journals, collections of letters and daybooks of the church architects and leaders, and many uncatalogued plans and drawings. Much of the written material deals with constructional and financial matters and contains little about style or meanings of the buildings. To supplement these manuscripts in the realm of interpretation, published writings and speeches by Mormon leaders, newspaper articles, and theological works are extremely valuable. Besides complete collections of LDS periodicals, newspapers, and books, the

Historian's Office maintains the Journal History, an indexed file of newspaper clippings on all aspects of Mormon history. Other journals and letters are available at the Utah State Historical Society, the Brigham Young University libraries, and at Southern Illinois University, Edwardsville, which has an extensive microfilm collection of documents relating to the Nauvoo period. I refer those interested in a more complete documentation of sources to my doctoral dissertation (University of Michigan, 1973) and for a succinct interpretive analysis of the nineteenth-century temples to David S. Andrew and Laurel B. Blank, "The Four Mormon Temples in Utah," *Journal of the Society of Architectural Historians*, 30, 1 (1971): 51–65. For an explanation of the organization of the present-day building committee and a description of the types of structures the Saints build today, see Martin Ray Young, "A Guide for Planning the Meeting House of the Church of Jesus Christ of Latter-day Saints," *American Institute of Architects Journal*, 39, 2 (1963): 51–56.

Chapter 3

Church leaders promised throughout the nineteenth century that the Saints would regain the property in Jackson County, Missouri, that was rightfully theirs and that the temple at Independence would eventually be completed. No specific time was appointed for its construction, but speeches by church officials implied that it would perhaps be during the millennium or just before. The Latter-day Saints still intend to build a temple at Independence but as yet have been unable to do so because they cannot obtain the deed to the entire original site consecrated by Joseph Smith. The Utah church owns about 40 percent of the temple lot. Another 40 percent belongs to the Reorganized Church of Jesus Christ of Latter Day Saints, based in Independence, a group founded in 1852 which disclaimed all association with the Saints under the leadership of Brigham Young. The remaining 20 percent, which includes the spot where Smith stood when he dedicated the ground, is owned by still another offspring of the original Saints. In 1859 Granville Hedrick organized the Church of Jesus Christ Temple Lot. The "Hedrickites," with about three thousand members, retain ownership of this portion; see Wallace Turner, *The Mormon Establishment* (Boston, 1966), pp. 42–43.

Joseph Smith's ideas about town planning influenced the layout of all future Mormon cities and towns, which followed the plat of Zion with its wide streets meeting at right angles and houses set back from the streets to allow for planting trees. See John W. Reps, *Town Planning in Frontier America* (Princeton, 1969), pp. 410–420; Joel E. Ricks, *Forms and Methods of Early Mormon Settlement* (Logan, Utah, 1964); Charles L. Sellers, "Early Mormon Community Planning," *Journal of the American Institute of Planners*, 28, 1 (1962): 24–30.

Besides the two sets of drawings for the Independence temple, there is another small group of drawing fragments belonging to either Kirtland or Independence. In July 1835 a man named Michael Chandler arrived in Kirtland with four Egyptian mummies and several rolls of papyri which he had been exhibiting across the country. The church purchased these objects and Smith began to translate the hieroglyphics, which he claimed to be the writing of Abraham and Joseph. The task proved too difficult, and he eventually turned to revelation. The result was the Book of Abraham, the story of the creation and the early history of the Hebrews, and it forms part of the *Pearl of Great Price*. For the significant differences between Genesis and Smith's version, see Fawn Brodie, *No Man Knows My History: The Life of Joseph Smith the Mormon Prophet* (London, 1963), pp. 170–175. The Book of Abraham influenced the development of theology at Nauvoo, and, consequently, the symbolism of the later temple. The papyri were sold after Smith's death and were presumed to have been destroyed in the great Chicago fire, when the Wood Museum, where they were housed, was burned. Only three facsimiles of the hieroglyphics were known until 1966, when a scholar working in Metropolitan Museum realized that a papyrus he was studying was identical to one of these facsimiles. The museum presented the church with eleven fragments of the papyri in 1967. Three of them were pasted on backing paper upon which were sketched portions of a ground plan of a building looking very much like Independence and Kirtland. These drawings do not provide any new information about either temple, since they show only a few rows of seats. Description and illustrations of the drawing fragments are to be found in an article in a church periodical, T. Edgar Lyon, "The Sketches on the Papyri Backing," *Improvement Era*, 71, 5 (1968): 19–23.

See Thomas E. O'Donnell, "The First Mormon Temple, at Kirtland, Ohio," *Architecture* 17, 2 (1924): 165–169, for a description of the building and its materials; also "Master Detail Series, Historic American Buildings: Kirtland Temple," *Architectural Forum*, 64, 3 (1936): 177–183.

The story of the Mormons at Kirtland and the disintegration of the community is related in Willis Thornton, "Gentile and Saint at Kirtland," *Ohio State Archaeological Quarterly*, 63, 1 (1954): 8–33.

Chapter 4

The history of the Nauvoo period is thoroughly explored by Robert Bruce Flanders, *Nauvoo, Kingdom on the Mississippi* (Urbana, 1965); illustrations and descriptions of some of the domestic architecture of Nauvoo, with brief mention of the temple, can be found in Robert M. Lillibridge, "Architectural Currents on the Mississippi River: Nauvoo, Illinois," *Journal of the Society of Architectural Historians*, 19, 3 (1960): 109–114.

A prodigious amount of research has been carried out by Nauvoo Restoration, Inc., a church-funded corporation based in Salt Lake City, whose interests lie in attempting to reconstruct the appearance of Nauvoo as it was when the Mormons resided there. Using photographs, newspaper accounts, letters, journals, and printed sources, as well as information from archaeological investigations, Nauvoo Restoration has arrived at an accurate idea of the appearance of the exterior and interior of the temple.

Mention should be made of the controversy between the Reorganized Church of Jesus Christ of Latter Day Saints and the Utah church over the question of the completion of the Nauvoo temple. The Reorganized Church has consistently maintained that the temple was not finished, while the Utah Mormons insist that it was built according to the designs of Smith and substantially completed before the Saints left Nauvoo. The essence of the quarrel is actually not over the building itself, but over the ritual which was instituted during this episode in the history of the Saints. The Reorganized Church denies that any ritual whatsoever took place in the temple and claims that Joseph Smith never took more than one wife. Their belief that the temple was not finished thus allows them to dismiss the doctrines and practices of the Utah church as fabrications of Brigham Young and to regard themselves as the continuers of the uncorrupted tradition of Smith. The Mormons, on the other hand (RLDS members do not call themselves Mormons), consider the completion and use of the temple to be proof that the rites practiced in Utah were divinely authorized by revelation to Smith. In my opinion, the unbiased observer must agree with the Utah church that the important parts of the temple were completed and functioning before the Mormons left for the west. The many contemporary descriptions of the temple and the eyewitness accounts of the endowment ceremonies dispel any doubt that these had become a part of Mormonism before the Saints had left Illinois.

Masonic symbols could have been seen not only in handbooks, but also in a wide variety of popular decorative arts. See Alan Gowans, "Freemasonry and the Neoclassic Style in America," *Antiques*, 77, 2 (1960): 171–175.

Chapter 5

For Utah architecture in general, see Paul Goeldner, *Utah Catalog-Historic American Buildings Survey* (Salt Lake City, 1969); for domestic architecture, the same author's "The Architecture of Equal Comforts; Polygamists in Utah," *Historic Preservation* 24, 1 (1972): 14–17.

Samuel H. Goodwin, *Mormonism and Masonry* (Washington, 1923), provides the most complete analysis (from the point of view of the Freemasons) of the relationship between Freemasonry and the Mormons. The Mormon attitude is presented in E. Cecil McGavin, *Mormonism and Masonry* (Salt Lake City, 1956). Richard V. Francaviglia, "The Mormon Landscape: Existence, Creation and Perception of a Unique Image in the American West" (Ph.D. dissertation, University of Oregon, 1970), p. 39, says, "Some years ago, before they were demolished, pure LDS symbolism could be seen on certain of those church buildings [Relief Society buildings, small endowment halls, ward chapels]. The earlier ward chapel, and small endowment hall were especially rich in symbols, such as the Beehive . . . the square and the compass, and other 'L' and 'V' symbols reminiscent of the Masonic order."

Phoebe Stanton, *The Gothic Revival and American Church Architecture* (Baltimore, 1968), chapter 2, discusses the castellated style. For examples of collegiate Gothic applied to ecclesiastical architecture, see Jacob Landy, *The Architecture of Minard Lafever* (New York and London, 1970), chapter 9, and W. H. Hunter, "Robert Cary Long, Jr., and the Battle of Styles," *Journal of the Society of Architectural Historians* 16, 1 (1957): 28–30.

Chapter 6

A comprehensive history of the Dixie Mission is given in Nels Anderson, *Desert Saints: The Mormon Frontier in Utah* (Chicago, 1966), while the place of the temples in the Mormon economic system is discussed briefly in Leonard

J. Arrington, *Great Basin Kingdom* (Cambridge, 1958), pp. 339–341.

Less is known about the later Utah temples than about Salt Lake City or the eastern temples. In 1938 Truman Angell's plan, elevation, and section for St. George were found in the temple, but there are no drawings for Manti and those for Logan are primarily interior details. In 1886 W. H. Folsom dictated a short autobiography, now in the Bancroft Library of the University of California at Berkeley, but he gave almost no information about his architectural work for the church. Truman Angell, Jr., also remains a shadowy figure.

American attitudes towards the wilderness are evaluated in two works by Perry Miller, *Nature's Nation* (Cambridge, 1967), and *Errand Into the Wilderness* (Cambridge, 1964); also Roderick Nash, *Wilderness and the American Mind* (New Haven and London, 1967), particularly chapter 2, and Hans Huth, *Nature and the American; Three Centuries of Changing Attitudes* (Berkeley, 1957). David C. Huntington, *The Landscapes of Frederick Edwin Church* (New York, 1966), proposes that millennial meanings can be found in the work of this nineteenth-century painter. Also of interest is Barbara Novak, "American Landscape: The Nationalist Garden and the Holy Book," *Art in America* (January–February, 1972): 46–57.

Bibliography

A. Writings of Joseph Smith

Smith, Joseph. The Book of Mormon [1830]. 1920 ed. Salt Lake City, 1968.
———. The Doctrine and Covenants of the Church of Jesus Christ of Latter-day Saints [1835]. 1921 ed. Salt Lake City, 1968.
———. *History of the Church of Jesus Christ of Latter-day Saints.* Edited by B. H. Roberts. 6 vols. Salt Lake City, 1908.
———. The Pearl of Great Price. 1921 ed. Salt Lake City, 1968.

B. Manuscripts, Documents, and Drawings

Bancroft Library, University of California, Berkeley. Dictation by William H. Folsom, Manti, 1886.
Church of Jesus Christ of Latter-day Saints Church Historian's Office. Autobiography of Truman O. Angell.
———. Truman O. Angell, Journal, 1851–1856, 1856–1857.
———. Truman O. Angell, Letters.
———. Truman O. Angell, Jr., Letters.
———. A Short Sketch of the Life of Harrison Burgess, Son of William and Violaty Burgess.
———. William H. Folsom, Letters.
———. Joseph Hall and Samuel Roskelly, The Temple of the Lord, Erected at Logan, Cache County, Utah. The History of its Construction from the Foundation to the Dome—A Description of the Sacred Edifice, 1877–1884.
———. Journal History.
———. D. M. McAllister and Bureau of Information, A Description of the Great Temple, Salt Lake City.
———. John D. McAllister, Reminiscences and Journal, 1827–1906.
———. Artemus Millett, Biography of Artemus Millett.
———. John Taylor, Letterbooks.
———. Uncatalogued drawings of the Independence, Nauvoo, Salt Lake, Logan, and St. George temples.
———. Brigham Young, Letterbooks.
———. Brigham Young, Manuscript History of Brigham Young, 1844–1877.

Clements Library, University of Michigan. Henry Halkett's Notes Upon Joe Smith the Prophet, 1844.

Huntington Library. Truman O. Angell, Letter to Brigham Young.

———. James G. Bleak, Historians Mem. Day Book, Southern Mission, 1871.

———. William H. Folsom, Specifications for Building Tower on St. George Temple.

———. E. L. Parry, Report to J. G. Bleak on the Building of the St. George Temple.

Southern Illinois University, Edwardsville. Microfilm Collection, Sources of Mormon History in Illinois, Hascall Family Letters.

Utah State Historical Society. Diary of Oliver Boardman Huntington, 1847–1900.

———. Guy M. Keysor, Autobiographies and Reminiscences, 1816–1851.

———. George Laub, Diaries, 1814–1880.

C. Theses and Dissertations.

Bilderback, James C. "Masonry and Mormonism, Nauvoo, Illinois: 1841–47." M.A. thesis, State University of Iowa, 1937.

Colvin, Don F. "A Historical Survey of the Mormon Temple at Nauvoo, Illinois." M.S. thesis, Brigham Young University, 1962.

Curtis, Kirk M. "History of the St. George Temple." M.S. thesis, Brigham Young University, 1964.

Fields, Clarence L. "History of the Kirtland Temple." M.S. thesis, Brigham Young University, 1963.

Fracaviglia, Richard V. "The Mormon Landscape: Existence, Creation and Perception of a Unique Image in the American West." Ph.D. dissertation, University of Oregon, 1970.

Larkin, Melvin A. "The History of the L.D.S. Temple in Logan, Utah." M.S. thesis, Utah State Agricultural College, 1954.

Stubbs, Glen R. "A History of the Manti Temple." M.S. thesis, Brigham Young University, 1960.

Swenson, Russell Brown. "The Influence of the New Testament Upon Latter-Day Saint Eschatology from 1830–46." M.A. thesis, University of Chicago, 1931.

D. Books

Anderson, Nels. *Desert Saints: The Mormon Frontier in Utah*. Chicago and London, 1966.

Andrews, Edward D. *The People Called Shakers*. New York, 1963.

Arrington, Leonard. *Great Basin Kingdom*. Cambridge, 1958.

Benjamin, Asher. *The Practical House Carpenter*. Boston, 1830.

———. *A Reprint of The Country Builders' Assistant, 1805, The American Builders' Companion, 1806, The Rudiments of Architecture, 1814, The Practical House Carpenter, 1832, and Practice of Architecture, 1833*. Edited by Aymar Embury II. New York, 1917.

Blum, Ida. *Nauvoo, American Heritage*. By the Author, 1969.

Bowles, Samuel. *Our New West*. Hartford, 1870.

Britton, John, and Pugin, A. *Illustrations of the Public Buildings of London*. 2 vols. London, 1825–1828.

Brodie, Fawn M. *No Man Knows My History: The Life of Joseph Smith the Mormon Prophet*. London, 1963.

Burton, Richard F. *The City of the Saints and Across the Rocky Mountains to California* [1861]. Edited with an introduction and notes by Fawn M. Brodie. New York, 1963.

Campen, Richard N. *Architecture of the Western Reserve, 1800–1900*. Cleveland and London, 1971.

Corrill, John. *A Brief History of the Church of Jesus Christ of Latter-day Saints (commonly called Mormons), Including an Account of Their Doctrine and Discipline, with the Reasons of the Author for Leaving the Church*. St. Louis, 1839.

Creer, Leland Hargrave. Utah and the Nation. Vol. VII of *University of Washington Publications in the Social Sciences*. Seattle, 1929.

Cross, Whitney. *The Burned-Over District: The Social and Intellectual History of Enthusiastic Religion in Western New York, 1800–1850*. Ithaca, N.Y., 1950.

Dick, Thomas. *Collected Works of Thomas Dick*. 2 vols. Philadelphia, 1843.

Dorsey, Stephen P. *Early English Churches in America, 1607–1807*. New York, 1952.

Dwyer, Robert J. *The Gentile Comes to Utah: A Study in Religious and Social Conflict (1862–90)*. Washington, D.C., 1941.

Early, James. *Romanticism and American Architecture*. New York, 1965.

Ferris, Benjamin G. *Utah and the Mormons*. New York, 1854.

Flanders, Robert Bruce. *Nauvoo, Kingdom on the Mississippi*. Urbana, Illinois, 1965.

Ford, Thomas G. *A History of Illinois*. Chicago, 1854.

Furniss, Norman F. *The Mormon Conflict, 1850–1859*. New Haven, 1960.

Gates, Susa Young, and Widtsoe, Leah T. *The Life Story of Brigham Young*. New York, 1930.

Gibbs, James. *A Book of Architecture*. London, 1728.

Gilchrist, Agnes A. *William Strickland, Architect and Engineer, 1788–1854*. Philadelphia, 1950.

Goeldner, Paul. *Utah Catalog-Historic American Buildings Survey*. Salt Lake City, 1932.

Goodwin, S. H. *Additional Studies in Mormonism and Masonry*. Salt Lake City, 1932.

———. *Mormonism and Masonry*. Washington, D.C., 1924.

Gowans, Alan. *Images of American Living*. New York and Philadelphia, 1964.

Green, Nelson Winch. *Fifteen Years Among the Mormons, Being the Narrative of Mrs. Mary Ettie V. Smith*. New York, 1858.

Hamlin, Talbot. *Greek Revival Architecture in America*. London, 1944.

Hansen, Klaus J. *Quest for Empire: The Political Kingdom of God and the Council of Fifty in Mormon History*. East Lansing, Mich., 1967.

Hardie, James. *The New Free-Mason's Monitor or, Masonic Guide*. New York, 1818.

Harrington, Virginia, and Harrington, J.C. *Rediscovery of the Nauvoo Temple: Report on the Archaeological Excavations*. Salt Lake City, 1971.

Hatcher, Harlan H. *The Western Reserve: The Story of New Connecticut in Ohio*. New York and Indianapolis, 1949.

Hirschson, Stanley. *The Lion of the Lord, A Biography of Brigham Young*. New York, 1969.

Hitchcock, Henry Russell. *American Architectural Books: A List of Books, Portfolios, and Pamphlets on Architecture and Related Subjects Published in America Before 1895*. Minneapolis, 1962.

———. *Architecture: Nineteenth and Twentieth Centuries*. 2nd ed. Baltimore, 1971.

Holloway, Mark. *Heavens on Earth: Utopian Communities in America, 1680–1880*. New York, 1951.

Hope, Thomas. *A Historical Essay on Architecture*. London, 1835.

Hopkins, John Henry. *Essays on Gothic Architecture*. Burlington, Vt., 1836.

Howe, Henry. *Historical Collections of Ohio*. Cincinnati, 1851.

Huntington, David C. *The Landscapes of Frederick Edwin Church*. New York, 1966.

Huxtable, Ada Louise. *Classic New York*. Garden City, N.Y., 1964.

Hyde, John. *Mormonism: Its Leaders and Designs*. New York, 1857.

Iwans, Anthony W. *The Relationship of Mormonism and Freemasonry*. Salt Lake City, 1934.

Kane, Thomas L. *The Mormons*. Philadelphia, 1850.

Kelly, J. Frederick. *Early Connecticut Meetinghouses*. 2 vols. New York, 1948.

Kilham, Walter H. *Boston After Bulfinch: An Account of its Architecture, 1800–1900*. Cambridge, 1946.

Kirker, Harold. *The Architecture of Charles Bulfinch*. Cambridge, 1969.

Lafever, Minard. *The Beauties of Modern Architecture* [1835]. Introduction by Denys P. Myers. New York, 1968.

Landy, Jacob. *The Architecture of Minard Lafever*. New York and London, 1970.

Langley, Batty, and Langley, Thomas. *Ancient Architecture Restored and Improved by a Great Variety of Grand and Useful Designs*. London, 1742.

———. *Gothic Architecture Improved by Rules and Proportions*. London, 1742.

Lewis, Henry. *The Valley of the Mississippi Illustrated*. Translated by A. Hermina Poatgieter, edited by Bertha Heilbron. St. Paul, 1967.

Linn, William Alexander. *The Story of the Mormons*. New York, 1902.

Ludwig, Allan I. *Graven Images; New England Stonecarving and its Symbols, 1650–1815*. Middletown, Conn., 1966.

Lundwall, N. B. *Temples of the Most High*. Salt Lake City, 1951.

Maass, John. *The Gingerbread Age; A View of Victorian America*. New York and Toronto, 1957.

McGavin, E. Cecil. *Mormonism and Masonry*. Salt Lake City, 1956.

———. *Nauvoo the Beautiful*. Salt Lake City, 1946.

———. *The Nauvoo Temple*. Salt Lake City, 1962.

Marshall, Walter G. *Through America, or Nine Months in the United States*. London, 1881.

Marx, Leo. *The Machine in the Garden*. New York, 1964.

Melcher, Marguerite F. *The Shaker Adventure*. Cleveland, 1960.

Miller, Perry. *Errand Into the Wilderness*. Cambridge, 1964.

———. *Nature's Nation*. Cambridge, 1967.

Morrison, Hugh. *Early American Architecture*. New York, 1952.

Mulder, William, and Mortensen, A. Russell, eds. *Among the Mormons: Historic Accounts by Contemporary Observers*. New York, 1958.

Nash, Roderick. *Wilderness and the American Mind*. New Haven and London, 1967.

Newcomb, Rexford. *The Architecture of the Old Northwest Territory*. Chicago, 1950.

Niebuhr, H. Richard. *The Kingdom of God in America*. Hamden, Conn., 1958.

O'Dea, Thomas F. *The Mormons*. Chicago, 1957.

Owen, Robert Dale. *Hints on Public Architecture*. New York, 1849.

Persons, Stow. *American Minds: A History of Ideas*. New York, 1958.

Prado, H. and Villapando, J. B. *In Ezechielem explanationes et apparatus urbis ac templi Hierosolymitani*. 2 vols. Rome, 1605.

Pugin, A. W. and Walker, T. L. *Examples of Gothic Architecture*. 3 vols. London, 1840.

Raynor, Wallace A. *The Everlasting Spires*. Salt Lake City, 1965.

Remy, Jules and Brenchley, Julius. *A Journey to the Great Salt Lake City*. 2 vols. London, 1861.

Reps, John. *Town Planning in Frontier America*. Princeton, 1969.

Richards, F. D. and Richards, S. W., eds. *Journal of Discourses by Brigham Young, His Two Counsellors, The Twelve Apostles, and Others*. 26 vols. Liverpool, 1854–1886, 4th reprint, 1966.

Roberts, Brigham H. *A Comprehensive History of the Church of Jesus Christ of Latter-day Saints, Period II*. Vol. VII. Salt Lake City, 1964.

Roos, Frank. *Writings on Early American Architecture*. Columbus, Ohio, 1943.

Rose, Harold W. *The Colonial Houses of Worship in America*. New York, 1963.

Sanford, Charles L. *The Quest for Paradise; Europe and the American Moral Imagination*. Urbana, Ill., 1961.

Silverberg, Robert. *Mound Builders of Ancient America*. New York, 1968.

Smith, Henry Nash. *Virgin Land; The American West as Symbol and Myth*. New York, 1950.

Smith, Lucy. *Biographical Sketches of Joseph Smith the Prophet 1853*. New York, 1969.

Smith, Timothy, *Revivalism and Social Reform in Mid-Nineteenth-Century America*. New York, 1957.

Snow, Eliza R. *Biography and Family Record of Lorenzo Snow*. Salt Lake City, 1884.

Southern Illinois University. *Sources of Mormon History in Illinois*. Carbondale, 1966.

Stanton, Phoebe. *The Gothic Revival and American Church Architecture*. Baltimore, 1968.

Talmage, James E. *Articles of Faith*. Salt Lake City, 1960.

———. *The House of the Lord*. Salt Lake City, 1968.

Taylor, P. A. M. *Expectations Westward: The Mormons and the Emigration of Their British Converts in the Nineteenth Century*. Ithaca, N.Y., 1966.

Todd, Jay M. *The Saga of the Book of Abraham*. Salt Lake City, 1969.

Tullidge, Edward W. *Tullidge's Histories of Utah*. 2 vols. Salt Lake City, 1889.

Tuveson, Ernest Lee. *Redeemer Nation; The Idea of America's Millennial Role*. Chicago and London, 1968.

Upton, Harriet Taylor. *History of the Western Reserve*. 2 vols. Chicago and New York, 1910.

Vallet, Emile. *Communism; History of the Experiment at Nauvoo of the Icarian Settlement*. Nauvoo, Ill., n.d.

Wait, Mary V. *Brigham Young in Cayuga County, 1813–1829*. Ithaca, N.Y., 1964.

Webb, Thomas Smith. *Freemasons' Monitor; or Illustrations of Masonry*. Salem, Mass., 1812.

West, Ray B. *Kingdom of the Saints*. New York, 1957.

Weston, Joseph H. *Mormon Architecture*. Salt Lake City, 1949.

White, Theo B., ed. *Philadelphia Architecture in the Nineteenth Century*. Philadelphia, 1953.

Wiebenson, Dora. *Sources of Greek Revival Architecture*. London, 1969.

Young, Brigham. *Discourses of Brigham Young*. Edited by John A. Widtsoe. Salt Lake City, 1925.

E. Articles

Andrew, David S. and Blank, Laurel B. "The Four Mormon Temples in Utah." *Journal of the Society of Architectural Historians*, XXX, No. 1 (1971), pp. 51–65.

Arrington, Joseph Earl. "Destruction of the Mormon Temple at Nauvoo." *Journal of the Illinois State Historical Society*, XL, No. 4 (1947), pp. 414–425.

———. "Nauvoo Sun Stone a Century Later." *Journal of the Illinois State Historical Society*, L, No. 1 (1957), pp. 99–100.

Bronner, Edwin B. "Quaker Landmarks in Early Philadelphia." *Historic Philadelphia; From the Founding Until the Early Nineteenth Century*. Vol. 43, Part I of *Transactions of the American Philosophical Society*. Philadelphia, 1953.

Brown, Ira V. "Watchers for the Second Coming: The Millennarian Tradition in America." *Mississippi Valley Historical Review*, XXXIX, No. 3 (1952), pp. 441–458.

Buckingham, J. H. "Illinois as Lincoln Knew It: A Boston Reporter's Record of a Trip in 1847." *Papers in Illinois History and Transactions for the Year 1937*. Springfield, 1938, pp. 109–187.

Chandler, John W. "The Communitarian Quest for Perfection." *Essays in Honor of H. Shelton Smith*. Edited by Stuart C. Henry. Raleigh, N.C., 1963, pp. 48–79.

Condit, Carl W. "The Mormon Tabernacle." *Progressive Architecture*, Vol. 47 (1966), pp. 158–161.

Cross, W. E. "Mormon Temple Plate." *Antiques*, LXVII, No. 1 (1955), p. 76.

Dahl, Curtis. "Mound Builders, Mormons, and William Cullen Bryant." *New England Quarterly*, XXXIV, No. 2 (1961), pp. 178–190.

Ferree, Barr. "Architecture." *Engineering Magazine*, VI, No. 1 (1893).

———. "Two Early Ohio Churches—Tallmadge Congregational Church; Claridon Church." *Architectural Record*, LVI (1924), pp. 286–288.

Gayler, George R. "The Mormons and Politics in Illinois: 1839–1844." *Journal of the Illinois State Historical Society*, XLIX, No. 1 (1956), pp. 48–66.

Goeldner, Paul. "The Architecture of Equal Comforts; Polygamists in Utah." *Historic Preservation*, XXIV, No. 1 (1972), pp. 14–17.

Goodman, Jack. "Way Down South in Brigham Young's Dixie." *New York Times*, August 24, 1969, sec. 10, p. 17.

Gowans, Alan. "Freemasonry and the Neoclassic Style in America." *Antiques*, LXXVII, No. 2 (1960), pp. 171–175.

Green, Dee F. "Field Report." *Nauvoo Excavation Field Report*. Office of Research and Projects, Southern Illinois University, n.p., n.d.

Hersey, George. "Replication Replicated, or Notes on American Bastardy." *Perspecta* 9/10, 1965, pp. 211–248.

Hunter, Milton R. "The Mormon Corridor." *Utah, A Centennial History*. Vol. I. Edited by Wain Sutton. New York, 1949, pp. 179–200. Reprinted from *Pacific Historical Review*, VII (1939).

Hunter, W. H. "Robert Cary Long and the Battle of Styles." *Journal of the Society of Architectural Historians*, XVI, No. 1 (1957), pp. 28–30.

Kimball, Stanley B. "Nauvoo." *Improvement Era*, LXV, No. 7 (1962), pp. 512–517, 548–551.

———. "The Nauvoo Temple." *Improvement Era*, LXVI, No. 11 (1963), pp. 979–984.

———. "The Nauvoo Temple: An Essay on its History, Architecture, and Destruction." *Nauvoo Excavation Field Report*. Office of Research and Projects, Southern Illinois University, n.p., n.d.

King, Hannah T. "Architecture." *The Contributor*, October, 1882, pp. 38–39.

Larson, Gustave O. "Federal Government Efforts to 'Americanize' Utah Before Admission to Statehood." *Brigham Young University Studies*, X, No. 2 (1970), pp. 218–232.

Lillibridge, Robert M. "Architectural Currents on the Mississippi River Frontier: Nauvoo, Illinois." *Journal of the Society of Architectural Historians*, XIX, No. 3 (1960), pp. 109–114.

"Logan Temple." *The Contributor*, Vol. V, No. 9 (1884), pp. 354–357.

Lyon, T. Edgar. "The Sketches on the Papyri Backings." *Improvement Era*, LXXI, No. 5 (1968), pp. 18–23.

Maddex, Diane. "Nineteenth Century Tabernacle in Utah Demolished for New Center." *Preservation News*, XI, No. 5 (1971), p. 3.

Marcombe, Joseph E. "Freemasonry at Nauvoo." *Journal of History*, Vol. X, No. 4 (1917), pp. 408–439.

"Master Detail Series: Historic American Buildings: Kirtland Temple." *Architectural Forum*, LXIV, No. 3 (1936), pp. 177–183.

Meeks, Carroll L. V. "Picturesque Eclecticism." *Art Bulletin*, XXXII, No. 1 (1950), pp. 226–235.

———. "Romanesque Before Richardson in the United States." *Art Bulletin*, XXXV, No. 1 (1953), pp. 17–33.

Melville, J. Keith. "Brigham Young's Ideal Society: The Kingdom of God." *Brigham Young University Studies*, LX, No. 15 (1963), pp. 3–18.

"Mormon Temple in Salt Lake City." *Illustrated London News*, June 13, 1957, p. 570.

"The Mormons." *Harper's New Monthly Magazine*, VI, No. 35, pp. 605–622.

Musser, A. M. "From the President's Party." *Juvenile Instructor*, XI, No. 10 (1876), pp. 106–107.

"Nauvoo Temple." *Daily Enquirer*, Provo, Utah, December 30, 1889.

O'Dea, Thomas F. "Mormonism and the Avoidance of Sectarian Stagnation: A Study of Church, Sect, and Incipient Nationality." *American Journal of Sociology*, LX, No. 3 (1954), pp. 285–293.

O'Donnell, Thomas E. "The First Mormon Temple, at Kirtland, Ohio." *Architecture*, L, No. 2 (1924), pp. 265–269.

"Recollections of the Nauvoo Temple." From the *Illinois Journal*, December 9, 1853. *Journal of the Illinois State Historical Society*, XXXVIII, No. 4 (1945), pp. 481–485.

Roos, Frank S. "Ohio, Architectural Cross-road." *Journal of the Society of Architectural Historians*, XII, No. 2 (1953), pp. 3–8.

"Salt Lake City Temple." *Harper's New Monthly Magazine*, August, 1884, p. 394.

Sellers, Charles L. "Early Mormon Community Planning." *Journal of the American Institute of Planners*, Vol. XXVIII, No. 1 (1962), pp. 24–30.

Smith, David E. "A Bibliography of Millennialism." *American Quarterly*, Vol. XVII, No. 3 (1965), pp. 535–549.

Thornton, Willis. "Gentile and Saint at Kirtland." *Ohio State Archaeological and Historical Quarterly*, Vol. LXIII, No. 1 (1954), pp. 8–33.

Todd, Jay M. "Nauvoo Temple Restoration." *Improvement Era*, Vol. LXXI, No. 10 (1968), pp. 10–16.

Whiffen, Marcus. "The Progeny of St. Martin-in-the-Fields." *Architectural Review*, Vol. C, No. 595 (1946), pp. 3–6.

Young, Martin Ray. "A Guide for Planning the Meeting House of the Church of Jesus Christ of Latter-day Saints." *American Institute of Architects Journal*, Vol. XXXIX, No. 2 (1963), pp. 51–56.

Zobell, Albert L. Jr. "The Manti Temple." *Improvement Era*, Vol. LXXI, No. 5 (1968), p. 61.

F. Newspapers, Periodicals, and Pamphlets.

Deseret News. Salt Lake City. Various issues, 1855–1893.

Ensign Temple Issue. Ensign, Vol. I, No. 1 (1972).

Evening and Morning Star. Independence, Missouri, and Kirtland, Ohio, June, 1832–September, 1834.

Gospel Reflector. Edited by Benjamin Winchester. Philadelphia, January 1–June 15, 1841.

Latter-day Saints' Messenger and Advocate. Kirtland, Ohio, October, 1834–September, 1837.

Latter-day Saints' Millennial Star. London. Various issues, 1840–1900.

McAllister, D. M. *A Description of the Great Temple, Salt Lake City*. 9th ed. Salt Lake City, 1929.

Nauvoo Restoration, Incorporated. *Nauvoo Temple, 1841–1865*. n.p., 1965.

Nibley, Hugh W. *What Is a Temple? The Idea of the Temple in History*. Provo, Utah, 1968. Reprint of an article in *Millennial Star*, Vol. CXX, No. 8 (1958).

Temple Souvenir Number. The Contributor, Vol. XIV, No. 6 (1893).

Temples and The Latter-day Saints. Special issue of *Improvement Era*. Salt Lake City, 1967.

Times and Seasons. Nauvoo, Illinois, July, 1839–February 15, 1846.